CAMBRIDGE LIBRARY COLLECTION

Books of enduring scholarly value

History

The books reissued in this series include accounts of historical events and movements by eye-witnesses and contemporaries, as well as landmark studies that assembled significant source materials or developed new historiographical methods. The series includes work in social, political and military history on a wide range of periods and regions, giving modern scholars ready access to influential publications of the past.

The British West India Colonies

Stephen Bourne (1791–1868) was a British civil servant who served as a magistrate in Jamaica between 1834 and 1841 and as Registrar of British Guiana between 1841 and 1848. His daughter Elizabeth Campbell left England with her father in 1834, and lived in the West Indies for thirteen years. This volume contains two essays and a published letter, the essays written by Elizabeth Campbell and the letter by Stephen Bourne, discussing the effects and limits of the Emancipation Act on the economy and society of the British West Indies. The two essays by Campbell discuss the limited social effects of the Emancipation Act, with the letter by Bourne suggesting ways to improve the economic prosperity of the West Indies. The ideology of later abolitionists, who endeavoured to improve social and economic conditions in plantations to demonstrate the possibility of prosperity without slavery, is fully explored in this volume.

T0382562

Cambridge University Press has long been a pioneer in the reissuing of out-of-print titles from its own backlist, producing digital reprints of books that are still sought after by scholars and students but could not be reprinted economically using traditional technology. The Cambridge Library Collection extends this activity to a wider range of books which are still of importance to researchers and professionals, either for the source material they contain, or as landmarks in the history of their academic discipline.

Drawing from the world-renowned collections in the Cambridge University Library, and guided by the advice of experts in each subject area, Cambridge University Press is using state-of-the-art scanning machines in its own Printing House to capture the content of each book selected for inclusion. The files are processed to give a consistently clear, crisp image, and the books finished to the high quality standard for which the Press is recognised around the world. The latest print-on-demand technology ensures that the books will remain available indefinitely, and that orders for single or multiple copies can quickly be supplied.

The Cambridge Library Collection will bring back to life books of enduring scholarly value (including out-of-copyright works originally issued by other publishers) across a wide range of disciplines in the humanities and social sciences and in science and technology.

The British
West India Colonies

In Connection with Slavery, Emancipation, etc.

ELIZABETH CAMPBELL
EDITED BY STEPHEN BOURNE

CAMBRIDGE
UNIVERSITY PRESS

CAMBRIDGE UNIVERSITY PRESS

Cambridge, New York, Melbourne, Madrid, Cape Town, Singapore,
São Paolo, Delhi, Dubai, Tokyo, Mexico City

Published in the United States of America by Cambridge University Press, New York

www.cambridge.org
Information on this title: www.cambridge.org/9781108020701

© in this compilation Cambridge University Press 2010

This edition first published 1853
This digitally printed version 2010

ISBN 978-1-108-02070-1 Paperback

THE

BRITISH WEST INDIA COLONIES

IN CONNECTION WITH

SLAVERY, EMANCIPATION,

ETC.

BY

A RESIDENT IN THE WEST INDIES FOR THIRTEEN YEARS.

WITH AN

INTRODUCTION AND CONCLUDING REMARKS

BY A LATE

STIPENDIARY MAGISTRATE IN JAMAICA.

LONDON:

THOMAS BOSWORTH, 215, REGENT STREET.

1853.

LONDON :

G. J. PALMER, SAVOY STREET, STRAND.

INTRODUCTION.

THE following pages were written in 1847 in British Guiana, and form part of a work which it was then intended to publish, in order to suggest means by which prosperity might be established in the West Indian Colonies.

The author had singularly favourable opportunities of becoming well acquainted with the evils which required to be removed, and the remedies to be applied, and she was desirous of treating the subject with that degree of calmness and moderation, which becomes a person who has no personal or party feelings to gratify, and who desires to allay animosities, and, as far as possible, to remove prejudices.

That slavery is a monstrous evil few persons who have been brought up in a free and Christian country will deny; but it is only due to our countrymen and women who hold property in the West Indian Colonies, which was at one time cultivated by slaves, to consider well the circumstances which might have given rise to their participation in slavery, and to admit and commend the readiness with which they assisted to emancipate their slaves, when the legislature and people of this country were prepared to help them in that great, beneficent, and necessary measure.

Shall we now leave them to struggle alone? Or, shall we not rather assist them by every means in our power to carry into full and prosperous effect the work to which we incited them, and in the results of which we take so deep an interest?

It is said that the West Indians have overcome their diffi-

culties, and that they are now well able to compete with the
slave-owners of Cuba and the Brazils. That may be very true
as regards the great capitalists, who have survived the wreck of
1848; but, is it true as to the mass of the proprietors? How
many estates have been abandoned? How many have passed,
at merely nominal prices, into the hands of creditors and mort-
gagees? And what, as regards real freedom, is the condition
of many thousands of those who have been made free by Act
of Parliament? What, if freedom has been firmly established,
is the meaning of the continued complaints of the "Anti-Slavery
Reporter," with regard to the indentures of Africans, forced
emigration obtained for the advantage of the few at the expense of the many, and the general want of a true representation of the people, either in the Parliament of the empire,
the Houses of Assembly, or the Councils of Government?

Was it real, or only a qualified, freedom that the late Lord
Grey, Lord Derby, Lord Glenelg, and the Parliament of England promised to all the inhabitants of our West Indian
Colonies as the result of emancipation? It is now too late
to say that the people are not fit for freedom. That should
have been considered before, if indeed it is a subject which one
man ought to consider in reference to another. If not fit, why
not? And then, who were most to blame, the enslavers or the
enslaved?

It is also an unquestioned fact that many thousands of
persons, especially in Jamaica and British Guiana, who in
1833 were slaves, have purchased for themselves freehold
estates, varying in extent from one to fifty acres; that they
have made up roads, effected drainage, built houses, and
planted provisions. The money wherewith to purchase these
estates must have been obtained by labour; and when it is
considered that the quantity of sugar now exported from the
British West Indian Colonies is greatly on the increase, and
that a great deal of labour has been abstracted from the estates
in order to apply it to the cultivation by the people of their
own freeholds, it cannot be doubted that freedom has on the
whole been very advantageous to the community. On the
other hand, the cultivation of cotton and coffee has greatly fallen

off, and in some of the most healthy parts of Jamaica hundreds of acres of coffee are at present in what is called *ruinate*.

Our object should have been from the first, and it should be now, to render the colonists in general prosperous, to strengthen the connexion between the general Government and the people of the Colonies, to improve the African race through the freed men and women in the British West Indies, and thus to convert the evils of slavery, now we have put an end to it, into the means of promoting freedom in other countries, and extending its blessings to Africa itself.

Why should not all the benevolent men and women of England unite to realise the anticipations of the great men who devoted their lives to the abolition of slavery, and the emancipation of the negroes ?

Why should not we assist the colonists in their present attempts to improve their manufactures, to render their countries healthful by drainage, and to substitute cattle and machinery for manual labour, wherever that may be practicable ?

Now that we have, at an enormous expense of money and labour, given freedom to the slaves, ought we to withhold our sympathy from those whose fortunes have been sacrificed as the result of attempts to carry into effect the wise and benevolent designs of the mother country ?

In the working out these objects many mistakes have been made by all parties and all governments; let us hope it is not too late to correct them.

LORD CARLISLE, than whom a more sincere patriot is not to be found, recently remarked " This is the question of the age ;" and the late LORD SEAFORD, who had resided in the colony, said, " The Almighty has done everything for us in Jamaica, but we have done little hitherto for ourselves."

LORD HOWARD DE WALDEN, and many other proprietors, have spared no expense to improve their estates in Jamaica, and to advantage the people, and some important discoveries have recently been made on his lordship's estates, and still more important ones by Mr. Bessemer, in the process of manufacturing sugar. It is, perhaps, impossible to overrate the value of these discoveries ; but it should not be forgotten that the slave-owners may avail themselves of them. If we allow them to get the start of us again, by the means of increased capital and improved machinery, it will hardly be fair to ascribe their prosperity to the advantage which they may be supposed to derive from slave-labour. I am persuaded this advantage has been greatly overrated, and that if capital were directed to thorough draining, the estates in British Guiana and the coast-lands of Jamaica, and the erection of public mills for the manufacture of sugar according to the new principle, in all the colonies, it would be found highly remunerative; that many of the small freeholders and former managers of estates would turn their attention to the cultivation of canes as well as provisions, thus forming a middle-class, and that in the profits of manufacturers and merchants, as well as those which would arise from leasing or selling their surplus lands to voluntary settlers, the land-owners would find their true interest. Neither can it be doubted, that the beautiful mountains of Jamaica might be advantageously settled and cultivated by Europeans, and that free labourers in abundance might be found, either in the United States or in China, to drain and plant with sea-island cotton, always in profitable demand, the coast-lands of British Guiana, Dominica, and Trinidad.

Have the patriots, philanthropists, and Christians of England well considered what might have been the condition of millions yet in slavery in America, Cuba, Porto Rico, the Brazils, and Africa, at this moment, if proper attention had been paid to our West Indian colonies, and our experiment there had been made as successful in every respect as it might have been?

I had the pleasure of some acquaintance with the late Mr. Wilberforce, Sir Thomas Fowell Buxton, and Mr. Joseph John Gurney, and no one can more highly estimate than I do, their benevolent and noble exertions. Would that they were living now, or that it was in my power to induce all who revere their memory, and glory in their labours, to devote their energies to the completion of the work which is yet to be done, and can only be effected by the united, wise, and benevolent exertions of those who yet live. When Messrs. Sturge, Lloyd, and

Hervey visited Jamaica, in 1837, they did me the honour of a visit, as did Mr. Thom, and the late Mr. Kimball, from the Northern States of America; and afterwards Mr. and Mrs. Candler, a deputation from the Society of Friends, in England. I cannot doubt that these true-hearted and enlightened friends of mankind, will take an interest in these pages, and that their continued and increased exertions in the cause may be safely relied on. They may not agree in all respects with the reasonings of the author, but they will, I am sure, appreciate her motives, and approve the candour, moderation, and courage, with which she has expressed her opinions.

Should the demand for the present publication justify it, that of the other parts of the work will speedily follow.

S. B.

Brixton, Surrey, Dec. 17, 1852.

RELATION

OF

JAMAICA AND OTHER COLONIES TO ENGLAND.

It has been frequently asked, Of what use are the colonies to England ? It may be that, as colonies, they are really of no advantage ; that could they protect themselves as independent states, so as to exercise their industry and develope their resources in a manner equally successful, they would confer the same benefits on the country by which they have been planted as they do at present. But were the colonies blotted out of the map of existence, there is little doubt that Great Britain itself would sustain a serious loss. If the British colonies are of no advantage to the mother country, we must apply the same principle to the colonies of other European states in regard to the countries from which they have sprung. We must remember that had colonization never taken place, neither the United States nor the South American Republics could have existed. The aboriginal inhabitants of the New World would then have been left in undisturbed possession of their native soil, and unless there was any inevitable destiny, arising from the laws of nature, to render their extinction certain, they would doubtless at this moment be enjoying that measure of happiness, which a freedom from the restraints of civilized life, and an absence of its privileges, might afford them. The Africans might still have been as free as the government of their own chiefs would have permitted ; or they might have been held in subjection by the Turks and

Arabs. Their law might have been the Koran, and their destiny
that of the Bedouin encampment, or the control of the Sultan
or his vicegerents.   We do not ask, at this moment, whether
the happiness of mankind would thus have been promoted. We
must believe that the Sovereign of the universe provides for
the welfare of His creatures ; that even the wicked are His
sword ; that He causes " the wrath of man to praise Him, and
that the remainder of that wrath He will restrain."   But the
question arises, Has the benefit derived from these distant
settlements been such as to repay the expenditure which has
been lavished in fostering their growth ; to make amends for
the lives which have been sacrificed to their sultry or insalu-
brious climates ; or to reward the nations of Europe for the
cost of blood and treasure employed in defending them, and in
settling the contests to which their possession has given rise,
and of which matters affecting their interests have been the
occasion ?

In the first place, we must consider that it is the duty of
every state to provide facilities for the subsistence and the
welfare of its members.   Unless this is the case, for what
purpose are laws and government necessary, or what object do
they serve ? Might we not as well dispense with their assistance
altogether, and act as our own separate inclinations or our
sense of justice and propriety may direct ?   The confusion to
which such a state of things would give rise might be more in
accordance with the nature of some minds, than the restraint
imposed by the laws of the most wisely ordered community.
But supposing it to be desirable that a settled form of government should be adopted, the protection of life itself is an
object to be consulted before that of property, or even liberty.
It is of little importance to individuals, whether they perish by
the knife of the murderer, or whether by the institutions of
society, they are reduced to such a state of destitution as to
encounter a more lingering fate from an absolute want of the
necessaries of life.   Now it is generally considered that the
more densely peopled countries of Europe do not contain
within themselves the resources sufficient for maintaining their
own population in such a state of comfort as they ought to

enjoy ; indeed, that, in particular instances, without procuring a supply from some other quarter, starvation is nearly
inevitable. And, this is the case after millions have abandoned
the homes of their fathers to obtain the means of subsistence
in another hemisphere. Had they not done so, we must
suppose, either that their descendants would never have existed,
or that, by pressing still further on the means of subsistence,
they would have increased in an incalculable degree the miseries
of destitution amongst those who have remained behind. But
if the present inhabitants of Great Britain can obtain the
necessaries of life within the country itself, why has so great
an anxiety been evinced that they might be permitted to supply themselves from other quarters ? From whence, then,
can an adequate supply be derived ? Scarcely from those
countries that are placed in circumstances similar to those of
Great Britain itself. They require what they can raise for the
support of their own inhabitants. It is in those thinly peopled
regions of the globe, where the land is far more than sufficient
for the maintenance of those who are located upon it, that we
may expect to find a superfluity of agricultural productions.
The inhabitants of such countries chiefly devote themselves to
the cultivation of the soil ; and it is more for their advantage
to receive manufactured articles from those places where the
density of the population, and accumulation of capital (only
to be found in countries which have been long inhabited), afford
facilities for the production of these manufactures, in exchange
for the food or the raw material which they are enabled to raise,
than to expend their time and ingenuity in ineffectual efforts to
supply themselves with those products of labour and skill, for
the creation of which their circumstances are not adapted.

But in applying these remarks to the West Indies, it is
necessary to admit that they are less suited to the raising of the
food, which the inhabitants of temperate countries require, than
other places, the climate of which more resembles that of
Europe. They are also less fitted than such portions of the
globe to become the habitation of the more destitute inhabitants
of the mother country, who, in removing to another soil, expect
to support themselves by actual labour. But they are in a high

degree capable of supplying many productions, which contribute greatly to the comfort of the inhabitants of Great Britain, and also the raw material necessary to, at least one, of the most important of its manufactures. It may be said that if the West Indies cease to yield these commodities, they can be procured on equally advantageous terms elsewhere. But are Cuba, Brazil, or the United States, capable of increasing their supply of sugar, coffee, or cotton, so as to make up for any deficiency in that which the West Indies can afford, without an extension of the slave trade ? The inhabitants of uncivilized countries usually spend that time, which is not required for providing for their actual necessities, in enjoying the shade of their forests, the coolness of their seas or rivers, or in pursuing the tedious process of their imperfect manufactures ; so that it would be necessary to introduce civilization amongst them before their labour, or their soil, could be made available to the purposes of Europeans. In countries so populous as China or India, the land appears to be barely sufficient for the support of its inhabitants : so that it could scarcely be appropriated to raising such agricultural productions as the inhabitants of Great Britain may require, without creating a deficiency of the means of subsistence likely to prove highly injurious to the native population. Unless, then, there are other countries combining the advantages of civilization with a greater abundance of fertile land than is necessary to supply the wants of their own population, it is still either to the free or the slave countries of the West Indies that Great Britain must look, chiefly, for sugar, for coffee, for cotton, and for other tropical productions. Admitting all that can be said in favour of free trade, it can scarcely be doubted from which of these two it is most desirable that the supply should be obtained.

But it has been shown that the colonies are also of importance to Great Britain, as affording to her superfluous population a habitation, in which, although they lose some of the advantages arising from a highly civilized state of society, they find a field in which to exercise their energies and their enterprize, and the means of providing for their own wants more advantageously than they might have been able to do had they remained at home, and also that they are enabled to labour more usefully to others, because possessing a greater command over those resources which the Almighty has provided for supplying the wants of His creatures, than they could have done where these resources had been already appropriated by others. Whether it is possible for the natives of cold countries to accommodate themselves to a tropical climate, to such a degree as to be able to encounter much exposure to the sun, or any arduous manual labour, consistently with their health and welfare, is usually regarded as a matter so doubtful, as not to warrant any conclusion in its favour, unless as the result of much observation and experience. But it can scarcely be denied, that there are parts of the West Indies, as the high lands of Jamaica, the sea coast of British Guiana (when properly drained and cultivated), and other places, in which Europeans, whose occupation requires only a moderate degree of exercise, and affords them the opportunity of being sheltered from the direct rays of the sun during the hottest part of the day, may, if they will only exercise a fair measure of caution, at least in the first instance, enjoy as much health as they could do in any part of the world. To those persons of delicate constitution, who suffer particularly from the severe cold of a northern winter, the change under such circumstances, might be highly beneficial. Now it is not only the labouring classes in the mother country who find it difficult to provide for themselves and their families those means of subsistence which are not merely called for by their absolute necessities, but suited to their previous habits, and to the station of society in which they have been accustomed to move. There is a class, above that of mere labourers, the number of which must increase as the general diffusion of education renders the candidates, for all those situations in which mental qualifications are required, rather than physical, more numerous. The changes which are taking place in the state of society, and which evince a disposition rather to provide for the actual necessities of the most indigent portion of the community, than to regard the interests of the higher and middling classes, whose welfare has hitherto been chiefly consulted, may possibly increase the number of persons unaccustomed to severe toil, who find it difficult to obtain employment. Now, if the number of actual labourers in the West Indies is found to be greatly deficient, there is little doubt that sooner or later a supply may be obtained from some tropical country, by plans less objectionable than most of those which have been hitherto adopted; or, the want of manual labour may be supplied by machinery. But to carry into effect improvements, which the altered state of society requires, a large amount of skill and intelligence is necessary. The great work to be accomplished, where the mass of the population are comparatively uninstructed, not only as regards literature, but in the arts of civilized life, and the conduct fitted to secure their happiness in a state of freedom, is so to direct and influence their minds, as to enable them to perform the duties that are expected from them in a manner likely to promote their own happiness and improvement, and the prosperity of the countries they inhabit. It is desirable they should see those operations that require skill and ingenuity performed by others, that they may be able to perform the same tasks themselves, when called upon to do so. There are doubtless many persons in the mother country, who, if they ascertained that they could find in the West Indies the means of comfort and respectability, and occupations suited to their habits and inclinations, would be inclined to remove thither, and in case of their doing so would exercise an influence highly beneficial to the community. The discussions which have taken place on the subject of slavery have probably had the effect of deterring many of the better classes from seeking to advance their fortunes by identifying themselves with a system, which has been so generally regarded as one of injustice and oppression. The effect of such impressions could not be otherwise than injurious to the negroes themselves, as it would tend to place them for the time under the control and influence of persons more indifferent to considerations of justice and humanity. There are other circumstances that have been extremely unfavourable to the character of the white population of the West Indies. One of the most injurious has been, that most of the persons connected with the management of estates have left their native country and their friends, together with those religious and moral influences which might have corrected their faults and improved their dispositions, at so early a period of life that it is scarcely possible that their principles should have acquired anything like steadiness. They have been separated, in a great measure, even from the more respectable society which the West Indies afford, and exposed to the worst examples; so that even if their characters were incapable of being ruined, their health very probably gave way, and an untimely grave was the only refuge afforded them from the difficulties and hardships of their situation. It is not very probable that respectable families would leave England, unless some security were afforded them for a comfortable subsistence on their arrival in the West Indies; but if the subject were to receive that attention which its importance demands, there is little doubt that, for the evils referred to, it might be possible to find a remedy.

Leaving, however, a consideration of the advantages which Great Britain, or its inhabitants, may derive from the possession of such colonies as the West Indies, it cannot be doubted that, in reference to the less favoured portion of mankind, the country has a destiny to fulfil. It cannot have been the design of Providence, that an island, occupying a position apparently so insignificant on the map of the world, should have obtained so mighty a dominion; merely, that its population might be supplied with the productions of every soil and climate in return for those manufactures which their skill and industry may enable them to produce: nor is it enough, that by settling themselves in the most distant regions of the globe, they succeed in forming flourishing states, where desolation or barbarism might otherwise have reigned. All these are only the means by which results of far greater importance are to be attained, and to these results the colonies are, in all probability, essential. Scattered as they are, they form citadels in the midst of regions hitherto almost unvisited by the lights of civilization, or the beneficent influence of Christianity. In these citadels everything that adorns and dignifies humanity should find a refuge and protection, from whence its influence may be extended amidst the surrounding darkness. They everywhere resemble the city set on a hill, which cannot be hid. How important is it that their affairs should be so regulated, as that the happiness of the human species may be promoted, and that every race and colour, and tribe, may regard their existence as a blessing, and not as a curse.

But for the accomplishment of these objects it is of importance to inquire, what kind of influence should be exerted by the mother country over the colonies generally, and the West Indies in particular ? It is necessary that the influence should be such, as to enable the people to exercise their own intelligence and energies, and to develope their own resources without being cramped and fettered by undue restrictions. At the same time there is a tendency to certain evils which, undoubtedly, require to be repressed and restrained. The difficulty is, how to exercise this restraint in a manner consistent with the principles of freedom and a due regard to the rights of all classes of society.

Some uncertainty prevails as to the relation in which the colonies stand to the Parliament and the Government of Great Britain. In Jamaica, where a greater disposition has been shown to assert what are maintained to be the rights of a colonial legislature, than in other parts of the West Indies, an opinion has prevailed, that the constitutional rights of the Crown are the same in a colony as in the mother country; but that the interference of Parliament is inconsistent with the liberties of the colonists. It is maintained that, according to the principles of the British Constitution, the consent of the representatives of the people is necessary to the passing of laws and the raising of taxes, but that the British Parliament represents the people of Great Britain and not the people of the colonies, and that, therefore, they cannot bind the colonists, without their own consent, expressed through their representatives. Several instances have, however, of late occurred, in which it has been thought necessary that Parliament should interfere, even with the internal affairs of the colonies; but the grounds on which this interference rests, or the cases in which it is justifiable, are still, in a great measure, undetermined. It would appear that where differences arise, either between the government and the people of a colony, or between different classes of the people themselves, so as to threaten the peace of the community, no means of settlement can be provided without the interference of Parliament. So long as the colonies are too weak to make any effectual resistance, this settlement will meet with submission; but if they yield, merely to force, without being convinced of the justice of what is demanded, the result can scarcely be beneficial, and may only produce a greater uneasiness in bearing a yoke, which they may attempt to shake off on the first favourable opportunity.

It may be, however, that the interference of Parliament, with reference to the colonies, resembles the decision of an impartial judge, or of a jury, capable of deciding on the merits of the case rather than the legislation that is exercised in the affairs of the mother country. It may be that where there is a representative assembly, this assembly possesses a right to legislate in regard to the internal affairs of the colony; but that this right may be forfeited by misconduct on their own part. If this be admitted, the colonists have only to act rightly and they will possess as great a security for their rights and liberties as the inhabitants of the mother country. They may even have this advantage, that by an appeal to an impartial tribunal they have a greater security for justice, than is possible where differences must be decided by force, in which case the stronger party is sure to gain the ascendancy.

It is not unnatural, however, that the governors of colonies, and the Government, should be desirous of exerting as great an influence over the colonial legislatures, as the latter exercise over the Parliament of Great Britain itself. Merely to carry into execution the laws of the colonies, without the privilege of altering or amending those laws, may not appear a very desirable task. But the manner in which any efforts of this kind are regarded by the inhabitants of the colonies will depend on the belief that is entertained as to the beneficial tendency of any proposed alterations. The colonists will insist upon having their own opinions on such subjects as certainly as the Parliament of the mother country. Indeed, in some cases, an apparent acquiescence in anything that may be proposed arises rather from motives of policy than from an honest conviction. It is possible that in those colonies where there is less of apparent submission, there is, at the same time, less of real disaffection, than in others, where it may be supposed that a greater satisfaction with the measures of Government is entertained.

The question then arises, whether, in case the colonists oppose changes that are really beneficial, it is right to enforce their acquiescence. It may be asked, what would be the effect if any force were employed in the mother country to procure the consent of Parliament to measures that the ministers of the Sovereign may regard as desirable ? What is usually the character of those persons who yield to force, what reason and persuasion will not induce them to concede ? But it is a matter of opinion what changes are fitted to promote the welfare of a community. Persons in a colony may be influenced by local prejudices or self-interest ; those at a distance may be unacquainted with the circumstances ; and the effect of the measures they propose may be very different to that which they have intended to produce.

Reference has sometimes been made to laws as being morally binding, chiefly in so far as they are regarded as engagements which cannot be broken or rendered invalid without the consent of all parties concerned. It need not appear disrespectful to her Majesty to suppose that such engagements cannot be set aside by the authority of the Crown, and without the free consent of the subject, because we find that the Almighty himself, as the Sovereign of the people of Israel, constantly refers to the covenant which He had made with Abraham. The ark, or chest, in which the tables of the law were kept, is constantly styled the ark of the covenant. Any disobedience was spoken of as being a breach of the covenant. This covenant was ratified by solemn engagements repeatedly made by the people themselves. On their entrance into the land, which had been promised on the condition of their obedience, they were called upon to choose whom they would serve ; and when the people replied that they would serve the Lord, Joshua addressed them in these words : " Ye are witnesses against yourselves that ye have chosen you the Lord to serve Him ;" and they said, " We are witnesses." " And the people said unto Joshua, The Lord our God will we serve, and His voice will we obey. So Joshua made a covenant with the people that day, and set them for a statute and an ordinance in Shechem." From this time we find that not a single new law was promulgated. All the subsequent revelations were intended to explain and enforce the old law. Even when the Messiah came into the world, it was said to be the design of the Almighty " to perform the mercy promised to our fathers, and to remember His holy covenant, the oath which he sware to our father Abraham." It was said expressly by Christ himself, " Till heaven and earth shall pass, one jot or one tittle shall in no wise pass from the law till all be fulfilled." Human laws must be liable to imperfection, and therefore from time to time require change ; but it can scarcely be conformable to any right principle that a change should be made simply by the authority of one of the parties concerned, and without the consent, or even with the forced acquiescence, of the other.

There is no doubt that considerations of this kind would tend to limit the authority which might be exercised for requiring the adoption even of good measures by the Government of Great Britain over the colonies. In regard to the abolition of slavery, the difficulty has been peculiarly manifested. Those who imagined that they were treated with injustice in having measures intended to effect this object forced upon them, were not likely to lend a very zealous co-operation in carrying out those measures, and it is probably on this account that so many difficulties have arisen, that so much loss has been experienced by the proprietors, and that so unsettled a state of things has prevailed in the West Indies. Although there are cases of manifest injustice, where an appeal to force is necessary, yet those who require willing agents for the accomplishment of their designs will fail, if, instead of attempting to produce conviction, they rely on that authority which a Government may be able to exercise to enforce their measures.

SLAVERY.

THE nation which has proclaimed that all men are born free and equal still retains in the most abject servitude a large proportion of her subjects. It is supposed that, having obtained Texas, she is desirous of still further adding to her slave dominions by the possession of Cuba. Even the inhabitants of Jamaica are beginning to be apprehensive that designs upon their freedom are entertained by this great Republic of the West. Such is usually the fate of extreme opinions. They are found to be impracticable, and involve those who maintain them in inconsistencies which render their sincerity questionable. It seems that the province of intellect is occupied by truths of an apparently opposite tendency, which must be confined within their proper limits, or they would invalidate one another, and prevent that harmony of intellectual and moral qualities which constitutes the perfection of human nature.

Is it true, however, that this perfect freedom and equality is inherent in the species, and that all the distinctions which exist are a violation of those natural laws by which the universe is governed ? How far the principle of equality is applicable to infants it is nearly impossible to ascertain, but it is certain that if this equality ever exists it does not last long. A difference of strength, of intellect, and of moral qualities, soon becomes apparent. This difference continues to increase until, of two children born at the same time, one may become a Milton or a Newton, and another may scarcely be capable of directing the most common affairs of ordinary life. Freedom is still less the portion of all mankind from their infancy. For many years they are entirely under the control of their parents, and in after life they are subject to a variety of influences which limit, if they do not destroy, that freedom which is said to be their natural inheritance.

But it does not follow that, because all are not free, freedom is not a blessing which all may seek to obtain, and which, according to the principle that we should do to others as we would have that others should do to us, it is right to use efforts to diffuse as widely as possible. If we can ascertain why this blessing has been denied to so large a portion of the human race, it may be less difficult to find the means of extending its influence, if we cannot immediately render it universal.

The question, however, arises, What is that kind of freedom which it is so desirable to seek? If we mean by freedom an absence of moral restraint, then doubtless the most uninstructed of mankind enjoy it in the highest degree. Their situation resembles that which is spoken of by the apostle, " I was alive without the law once." Such is probably the condition of children during the earliest periods of their existence; and a state in which there is a complete absence of civilization may be regarded as the infancy of nations. We do not know that such a state is inconsistent with a certain measure of happiness, but it is happiness of an inferior kind, elevating men but little above the inferior creation. It would appear that so soon as Europeans visit the countries in which such races exist, this kind of freedom and this degree of happiness speedily vanish. It is not the African slave trade and slavery which are in fact the only or the greatest injuries inflicted by civilized nations on untutored savages. The Indians who peopled the New World on the arrival of Columbus have in some instances disappeared altogether, in others they are fast diminishing. From the wars of which we hear between the British and the Caffres at the Cape of Good Hope, with the aborigines in New Zealand, between the French and Tahitians in the South Seas, there is reason to fear that the work of extermination is still going on. Even where no intentional injustice seems to be perpetrated, the unhappy natives, on obtaining the fire-arms or intoxicating drinks of Europeans, appear to use them for their own destruction. Why is it that the intercourse of professedly Christian nations with the uninstructed part of mankind has been hitherto productive of so much crime and misery, and so little benefit? Do they believe that they are divinely authorised to treat those who have been less favoured than themselves as the Israelites were commissioned to treat the idolatrous natives of Canaan? Does not that religion which proclaims that there is neither Greek nor Jew, Barbarian, Scythian, bond nor free, require that

c 2

a different system should be adopted—a system of mercy rather than of judgment—a system that may save and not destroy ? The races that have passed away cannot be restored to existence, but for those who remain there may still be hope. Amongst these, the emancipated negroes in the British West Indies are probably placed in the most favourable circumstances, and have before them the greatest prospect of improvement.

As it is not the freedom of savage life which affords any security for permanent happiness, neither is it the freedom of the destitute and neglected classes in the mother country which is particularly desirable. We may suppose two persons alone in a remote island—for instance, Robinson Crusoe and his man Friday. The former might have said to the latter, " You are my servant. I regard you as my property, and maintain that I have a right to your labour. It is both my interest and my duty to afford you what is necessary to subsistence ; but should you act in opposition to my directions, I shall inflict such chastisement as may be necessary to bring you to a sense of your obligations." Or he might have said, " You are a free man. You may work for me or not, as you think proper ; but this island belongs to me. Whilst I am satisfied with your conduct I shall remunerate you for your labour, but unless you work for me, and accommodate yourself to my wishes, I cannot afford you subsistence ; and if you take anything without my consent, I shall regard it as a robbery, and punish you accordingly." It is clear that the master would possess as great an authority in the one case as in the other. The fear of want would operate as strongly on the mind of the free labourer, as the fear of the lash or any similar punishment on the mind of the slave. Neither the right to the soil, nor the right to inflict chastisement, could be maintained without some superiority, mental or physical, or some foundation in a sense of duty which might enforce the claims of the one over the other. If it were a matter of choice which system should be adopted, there are some persons who might prefer a claim to subsistence, even if attended with a liability to punishment, to a prospect of destitution in case of old age, sickness, or other incapacity for labour. Parents chastise their children, and in doing so they may exercise undue harshness and severity, but they would be regarded as unnatural were they to abandon them to want. Schools are conducted on the principle that a regular discipline ought to be maintained, and enforced by some kind of chastisement or correction. Whatever may be the faults of such institutions, they are regarded as preferable to total neglect. The great advantage possessed by the free labourer in a country like England is that he has a choice of masters; but the master has also a choice of servants, which is perhaps of more importance, where there are a greater number of labourers than can easily obtain employment. The liability to destitution which is attendant on a state of freedom accompanied with a scarcity of the means of subsistence may be mitigated, either by voluntary charity, or by the state supporting such of its members as need its assistance : but this support is seldom unconnected with circumstances of degradation which give it the character of a punishment. Even amongst the educated classes, those who are not rendered independent by the possession of property are compelled, by the fear of losing their station in society, and other evils, not only to labour with great assiduity, but also to consult the inclinations of those who are in more favourable circumstances than themselves, and to submit to numberless mortifications from the supposed inferiority of their position.

These references are not made for the purpose of justifying West Indian slavery, but in order to show that there are other forms of oppression which require equally to be guarded against. It is one thing to abolish slavery, and another to establish a good state of society in its place. The freedom which it is desirable to attain is something higher and nobler than the mere absence of corporal punishment :

> " 'Tis liberty of heart derived from heaven,
> Bought with His blood, who gave it to mankind,
> And sealed with the same token."

Indeed, to confer freedom on the slave, is to carry into effect the purest and most benevolent principles of Christianity. It is emphatically His work, who came to proclaim liberty to the captive, and if men are to be the agents in this work, it cannot be expected that they will succeed, unless by following the directions, and being guided by the example, of the great author of true freedom. The apostles in comparing the Christian religion with that by which it was preceded, constantly speak of the one as a system of bondage, the other of freedom. The Jews affirmed that they were Abraham's seed, and were never in bondage to any man, but they were told that they still required to be made free. Now there is an alphabet in religion as well as in literature. These exalted principles of freedom were not revealed to the human race until some thousands of years had been spent in preparing the way, by a development of those truths which required assent, before a still further advancement in light and knowledge could be attained. And when the revelation was actually made, how few there were who could receive or comprehend its import! There was a constant tendency to revert to that system which contained in a greater degree the principle of accommodation to the tendencies of unimproved human nature. There was a perpetual disposition to appeal to the fears of mankind, rather than to their hopes and their affections. Had not this been the case would nations professing Christianity have resorted so constantly to wars and persecutions of every kind that human ingenuity could devise, not only with a view to objects of worldly interest, but for the purpose of enforcing what they believed to be the true religion? In this respect Catholics and Protestants appear to have been very ignorant of the spirit of the religion they professed. Never were these tendencies more strongly manifested than in the civil wars in England, which led to the execution of Charles I. and the establishment of the Protectorate. Writers of later times who have discovered that Christianity is not a religion to be enforced by war and bloodshed, have charged with hypocrisy those religionists of former times, who had not become acquainted with this fact. But a little inquiry may serve to show that their views were not so totally unsupported by Scripture, as to prevent their being sincerely entertained. Miracles of the most appalling character had taught the Jews to regard their Divine Ruler as a Judge, who would severely punish any infringement of his laws, and they were required, in

numerous instances, as in putting to death idolaters, themselves to become the executioners of those by whom these
laws were disobeyed. It was not therefore very unnatural to
conclude that what the Almighty had at any time required
must be right; and to overlook the different circumstances in
which the promulgation of Christianity had placed the whole
human race. It was during this period, when religion was
regarded as a matter of supreme importance, in defence of
which life and every worldly interest ought to be sacrificed,
and whilst there still prevailed a great degree of obscurity as
to what the Creator really required, that the most important
colonies of the New World were acquired, and the introduction
of slavery was but one manifestation of the spirit of the times.

A reference to the conquest of Jamaica may render this
more apparent. Cromwell informed the Parliament that the
Spaniard was their natural enemy, "by reason of that enmity
that is in him against whatever is of God." Milton justified
the expedition to the New World, on the ground that it was
necessary to punish the Spaniards for their cruelties to the
Indians. The following language was addressed by the Protector to Vice-Admiral Goodson, at Jamaica: "It is not to be
denied but the Lord hath greatly humbled us in that sad loss
sustained at Hispaniola. But yet certainly his name is concerned in the work. You are left there, and I pray you set
up your banners in the name of Christ, for undoubtedly it is
his cause. The Lord himself hath a controversy with your
enemies; even with that Roman Babylon, of which the
Spaniard is the great under-propper. In that respect, we
fight the Lord's battles; and in this the Scriptures are most
plain." In a letter to the Governor of Barbadoes, desiring
him to encourage people to remove from that island to Jamaica,
after referring to the disasters which had been experienced
through the disposing hand of God, he adds, "Yet is not this
cause the less his, but will be owned by him, as I verily
believe, and therefore we dare not relinquish it; but shall, the
Lord assisting, prosecute it with what strength we can, hoping
for a blessing for his name's sake." It may be said that such
expectations, if they were ever sincerely entertained, have not

been realised. Let the present state of Jamaica show. It was nearly impossible that the cultivation of the island could be carried on without labourers accustomed to a tropical climate, and these were unhappily procured by means of the slave trade, which had previously existed. Many persons who might have thought it unjustifiable to make free people slaves, would probably consider that to purchase those who had been already deprived of their freedom and brought across the Atlantic, was only placing them in a situation favourable to their moral and religious improvement. Having obtained a right of property in the people, it was in conformity with the principles everywhere maintained by the Puritans, to place them under a discipline somewhat harsh and severe. In referring to the misconduct of the army, Cromwell enjoined upon Major-General Fortescue, then in Jamaica, "so to govern, for time to come, as that all manner of vice may be thoroughly discountenanced, and severely punished; and that such a frame of government may be exercised, that virtue and godliness may receive due encouragement." There is little doubt that the same course would have been recommended in regard to the negro slaves.

A change, however, speedily took place in the state of public feeling in England. The Independents, who obtained so great an influence under Cromwell, by insisting on the right of every separate congregation to choose its own minister, prepared the way for a system of universal toleration. If the right of choice rested with the people, a system of force and coercion on the part of the rulers, even for the purpose of propagating the true faith, could not be justifiable. The Protector recommended the Parliament to " be merciful, as well as orthodox." George Fox and his adherents used their utmost efforts to convince the inhabitants of every part of Great Britain, that war and Christianity were totally incompatible, and that force should in no case be employed for the support of religion. The son of Admiral Penn, who conducted the fleet by which Jamaica was captured, adopted Quaker opinions, and became the founder of Pennsylvania. It is true that principles of arbitrary government were maintained in England after the Restoration; but it was a government, which, although inflicting martyrdom and every species of injury and privation on the friends of civil and religious liberty, encouraged and sanctioned the utmost latitude in regard to every question of morality. With such a government, it would be a matter of little importance, whether slavery was in accordance with Christianity. It was quite enough that it was found to be profitable. Even supposing that the inhabitants of Jamaica and other parts of the West Indies had been convinced that slavery and the slave trade ought to be discontinued, they could not act in accordance with their convictions, unless they could have obtained the consent and co-operation of the government, nor could they prevent persons from settling amongst them and acquiring an influence in their legislative assemblies, and in every possible way, who considered that African labourers were merely to be regarded as cattle, and every kind of oppression justifiable, that tended to advance their own interests. What then were they to do? Were they to abandon the negro slaves, of whom they had already become possessed, to the tender mercies of those who would oppress them far more than themselves, or were they to persevere in endeavouring to improve their condition, in affording them all the protection in their power, and in using their efforts to mitigate, if they could not entirely remove, the hardships of slavery? If those who adopted this course were involved in numerous errors by the difficult circumstances in which they were placed, this need not occasion surprise. We should rather look to the results which are at present manifested. We should consider that the free negroes of the British West Indies almost universally possess some degree of acquaintance with the truths of Christianity; that numbers amongst them are in the habit of reading the Scriptures, and attending places of worship; that they are adopting the improvements of civilized life, and that there is great reason to hope for their further advancement. The evils of slavery may have been even greater than the most determined abolitionists have represented, but it is doubtful whether many of these evils could have been prevented under any circumstances, where so large a proportion of the population had until very lately been totally uninstructed in the principles of religion and morality. A system of force and punishment seems to be adapted rather to render the evil apparent than to provide the remedy. A reference to the Old Testament Scriptures will show that this was the effect even of the divinely appointed legislation of Moses. If we admit such a system to be in any case justifiable at the present day, we should endeavour as speedily as possible to have recourse to milder and better principles. An inquiry into the difficulties with which such a change would naturally be attended, and the efforts by which they have been, to a certain extent, overcome, will now engage attention.

EMANCIPATION.

FROM the manner in which the subject of slavery has been discussed in the mother country, it would appear that some of those benevolent persons who have taken so lively an interest in the welfare of the African race, have overlooked the fact that the question of freedom or slavery depended very much on the character and disposition of the slave as well as on those of the master. Probably there was never an instance in which tyrants were not found where there were people willing to be slaves. Now the slave is one who does not act according to his own convictions of what is right, but who submits to be controlled by another. There is, however, a kind of influence which persons of superior intelligence may exercise over others, which does not constitute slavery. That acquiescence which is yielded as the result of conviction, is by no means inconsistent with freedom. But a yielding to force without being convinced of the propriety of what is demanded, partakes, more or less, of the nature of slavery. It is necessary, however, before persons can judge for themselves of the course which it is right to adopt, that they should have some standard by which to regulate their conduct. No doubt the African negroes have some natural consciousness of their duties one to another, but their ideas on such subjects are usually so indefinite and imperfect, that, when they come in contact with Europeans, they are inclined to take it for granted that whatever is required of them must be right, although in opposition to the course which they would have adopted if left to themselves. They require then to be instructed in those principles of right and wrong which civilization and Christianity have rendered generally prevalent in countries which are subject to their influence. But, in the first instance, they do not understand the language of their masters, so that any intellectual communication is nearly impossible. Even when this difficulty is overcome, the absence of that reflection which requires to be called into exercise by mental cultivation, prevents them from deriving that benefit which might be expected, although efforts are actually made to explain to them the truths of religion and the precepts of morality. In addition to this, habits require to be formed, and it is not necessary to state that this is by no means an easy task. It is scarcely rational to suppose that so general a system of punishment has been adopted from a mere desire to inflict suffering, but simply because it was easier to acquire an influence in this way than in any other. The authority of the masters has been usually exercised through the head men, and it is well known that Africans when they attempt to exert authority are very ready to resort to force, probably from an inaptitude either in reasoning or appealing to any moral principle.

Undoubtedly the great difficulty is to find persons who will devote themselves to the improvement and civilization of their fellow-creatures, and these of a different colour and class to themselves. Such as have left their friends and relatives behind them in Great Britain, are inclined to regard their residence in the West Indies as a kind of banishment, from which they are anxious as soon as they can to escape. To obtain the means of doing this, they require as much labour as the people can be induced to give, and at the least possible expense. Many who leave their native country in early life, being removed from those influences which might have rendered them respectable members of society, adopt courses that can only end in their own degradation and ruin. A large number of the proprietors of estates reside in England, and whilst they have been accustomed to receive an income from their distant possessions, have imperfect information as to the best means of promoting the welfare of those from whose labour their income has been derived. Missionaries usually exercise a powerful influence on the minds of the people amongst whom they labour, but there are many circumstances of every day life with which it is scarcely possible that a minister of religion should interfere, or in regard to which it can be supposed that he will be rightly informed.

Another great obstacle to the change from slavery to freedom is, that as it is known that only those persons who are in a state of great ignorance or moral degradation, are willing to continue slaves, it becomes the interest of their owners to keep them in that state, that they may retain them as property. There is little difficulty in maintaining a right of property in horses and cows, but even the horse must be watched and guarded, skilfully trained and managed, or it will sometimes show a disposition to assert its natural liberty. The steam-engine will make no attempts of the kind, nor is it necessary to make laws to prevent cattle and steam-engines from being taught to read! The most absurd opinions might be propagated as to the rights of cattle and the inanimate creation, without exciting any apprehension that the rights of property would thus be endangered. The masters may find it advantageous to instruct their slaves in those mechanical arts which enhance their value as property, but to give them that knowledge which ennobles and dignifies human nature, would prevent them from being property much longer.

Now the treatment which is most successful for the enforcement and perpetration of slavery, unfits the slave in the greatest degree for the performance of the duties which a state of freedom renders necessary both to his own happiness and that of his family, and also to the welfare of the community of which he is a member. So that he is first of all degraded, or at least obstacles are placed in the way of his improvement, and this degradation is then urged as a proof of his incapacity for freedom, and a reason for rendering his servitude perpetual. If an inquiry were made into the real state of different parts of the

British West Indies, it would probably be found that, in those places where the greatest efforts have been made for the moral and intellectual improvement of the people, slavery has been a source of the greatest annoyance and dissatisfaction, and freedom the most successful.

The effects produced by slavery on the minds of the white inhabitants of the West Indies, were also a great hindrance to the successful establishment of freedom. A population comparatively uninstructed, cannot be expected to rise in intelligence and civilization, unless they are influenced and guided by those who are already in possession of the advantages which it is desirable to communicate to them. But that this influence may be exerted in a manner consistently with freedom, a habit of self-restraint on the part of the superior classes is required. It is necessary to appeal to the reasoning faculties, to adopt a conciliatory and persuasive mode of exercising authority where authority is justifiable, and to refrain from its exercise where it is inconsistent with the rights of the people. But slavery, by rendering the will of the master a supreme law which must always be obeyed, destroys these habits of self-restraint. It is a system which can only be supported by an appeal to force, whenever there is resistance on the part of the inferior, and this force must be proportioned, not to the justice of the case, but to the degree of resistance which has to be overcome. Those who have been accustomed to settle every question between themselves and their dependents by an infliction of punishment find that the adoption of any other course involves a change in their previous habits, which it is extremely difficult to make. They irritate where they cannot control, and create an impression on the minds of their inferiors that they are desirous of acting in a way injurious to their interests, but that they merely want the power. Any limits which may be imposed on the authority of the master in a slave country, or which the master from prudence, a sense of duty, or benevolence, may choose to impose upon himself, are an approach to the principles of freedom.

But the question as to how the pecuniary interest of the master in the slave required to be disposed of was a point of great importance in reference to emancipation. It may elucidate the subject to inquire into the nature of that claim to the labour of others, which constitutes one of the predominant features of slavery, and whether it may be advanced in any instance without injustice. We may suppose an island in the Pacific recently visited by Europeans, in which the inhabitants had subsisted for ages on the spontaneous productions of the earth, without clothing, without tools, without habitations, affording them a sufficient shelter, and without the means of intellectual improvement. Benevolent individuals might think proper to supply them with all these advantages, but the people themselves, although willing to receive them when offered, might not be so much aware of their value, as to work beforehand so as to obtain them. They might make engagements to labour afterwards so as to repay to those who had interested themselves in their welfare the expense which had been incurred for their benefit. Should they afterwards neglect to perform these engagements, they would, according to all the laws of civilized society, become liable to the enforcement of the obligations in which they had involved themselves. Had they merely received the advantages offered them with the knowledge that payment would afterwards be demanded they would have no right to complain that they were treated with injustice by the enforcement of this payment. But whilst labouring to perform their obligations they would require the means of subsistence from day to day, and should this be continally supplied, a fresh debt would be incurred, which they might never be able to discharge ; in such a case they could only be released from a state which would be, in effect, one of slavery, by a voluntary abandonment of the claim on the part of those who had at first assisted them, or by the payment of the debt by some other party. Many persons in England may suppose that the slaves in the West Indies owed to their masters nothing but injuries. This could only be decided by inquiring into the treatment which had been received in each particular case.

But supposing that the British Parliament would have been justified in abolishing slavery without granting any amount of compensation to the West Indian proprietors, or that these pro-

prietors had felt themselves called on to relinquish their supposed right of property in the people from motives of philan-
thropy and justice, we may inquire what would most probably
have been the result ?   The slaves were formerly supported in
part by the produce of that portion of the estates which was
allotted for their maintenance, and partly by supplies of clothing,
salt-fish, and other things which they received from time to time.
Labour was not obtained in consequence of a knowledge that
the necessaries of life could not be acquired in any other way,
but because idleness was regarded as an offence for which punishment would be at once awarded.   Now, so soon as the power
of inflicting this punishment was taken out of the hands of the
master, some other means of inducing the people to afford their
labour were required, or the cultivation of the estates could not
be carried on ; in other words, the payment of wages which
could be proportioned to the quantity of the work performed
was necessary.   There were many circumstances which affected
the price of labour besides the ability of the proprietor to pay
wages ; and in order to obtain labour even at the lowest price
which the people were willing to take, a large amount of capital
was required.   So far from having a sufficient capital in hand
to meet the exigencies of the case many owners of estates were
in circumstances of great embarrassment.   The opinion seems
now to prevail very generally that it is for want of capital both
to pay wages and to make the improvements called for by the
altered state of things, that there is so great a depression in the
state of West Indian affairs ; and would not the deficiency of
capital have been much greater if no compensation had been
awarded ?   Would not the condition of the labourer have been
far less favourable than it is if the proprietor had been destitute
of the means of providing for those expenses to which the
change of circumstances had given rise ?   The means of purchasing land, of obtaining better clothing, of building places
of worship, of supporting ministers of religion, have been
derived from the wages paid for labour on estates, and, in effect,
to a great extent from the compensation granted by Parliament.

But great as are the difficulties which might be expected to
attend a transition from slavery to freedom, they have been

already surmounted to such an extent as that there is the greatest encouragement to perseverance in encountering those which yet remain, and the greatest hope that in the end all doubts will be removed as to the superiority of freedom over slavery in promoting alike the happiness and the moral dignity and elevation of the species. A short review of the means that have been adopted may not be out of place.

It would be difficult to ascertain at what period the first efforts were made for at least preparing the negroes in the West Indies for freedom, if not of making them actually free. The earliest history of most nations is found to be involved in obscurity ; and this is already the case to a great extent with those territories which have been settled by Europeans in the New World, notwithstanding that their origin is comparatively recent. Those undertakings which have been of the greatest importance to the welfare of the human race, in their commencement often resemble the acorn, which, falling from some patriarch of the forest, is trodden under foot, and appears by the merest chance to escape annihilation, but which produces a tree that becomes the wonder and the admiration of the descendants of those who have passed over the spot where it first began to germinate without observing its existence. Imagination may picture the first efforts to call into exercise the untutored faculties of the African slave, but no record remains of the manner in which they were made. Probably the first important step to this improvement in the British colonies was the acquirement of the English language. This would open the way for a government of reason rather than of force. Another approach to freedom would be a recognition on the part of the master of the right of the slave to ever so small a portion of time, and a respect for the property which his industry during this time had enabled him to acquire, as well as a disposition to protect this property from being intruded on by any invader. Another step was allowing to women either the whole or a part of their time, according to the number of their children, thus enabling them to exercise that care over them which they could not do if required to labour incessantly for the master. Everything that had the effect of defining the rights and duties of the slaves by law, instead of leaving them entirely subject to the arbitrary caprice of the master, would enable them to acquire a knowledge both of what they had to expect and what was expected from them, so as to relieve them from that apprehension and uncertainty which must exist in the minds of those who are entirely dependent on the will of a single individual. Every opportunity afforded to the slaves of appealing to a third party for protection; every limitation of the master's authority to inflict punishment, would have a beneficial effect on their circumstances. There is little doubt that measures of this kind were adopted even before the condition of the slave had attracted much attention in England. Whatever facilities were afforded to missionaries to settle amongst them, together with every other means of religious improvement which they possessed, was of the greatest importance to their welfare. It is perhaps impossible to ascertain why the benevolence of Wilberforce, Clarkson, and others, should have been exerted to so great a degree in this direction. From the constancy and perseverance with which cases of oppression and injustice were brought before the attention of the British public, it is possible that the situation of the negroes was believed to be one of more unmitigated hardship than was really the case; but there is little doubt that a great service was rendered to humanity, as the pecuniary interest of many parties in England might have prevented any effectual remedy, had not the humanity of the people generally been strongly enlisted in the cause; and the colonists had scarcely the power, if they had the inclination, to make that decided change which circumstances rendered absolutely necessary. There is reason to think that a greater dissatisfaction with slavery existed amongst the white people themselves, at least in some parts of the West Indies, than many would be disposed to imagine. Prudence would be likely to prevent the expression of such sentiments, however strongly they might have been felt, from the fear of producing a total disorganisation in so unsettled a state of society. Whatever might have been the state of things in other colonies, the negroes in Jamaica, at the commencement of the apprenticeship, possessed property in horses, donkeys, goats, poultry, &c.

D

Some of them had considerable sums in money, and trinkets of
some value. They were in the habit of disposing of their
provisions so as to procure clothing which enabled them to
make a respectable appearance on Sundays, as they attended
in large numbers at their places of worship. But so long as
slavery continued, any interference on their behalf, together
with the degree of security they enjoyed in the possession of
their grounds, rendered them the more independent of the
authority of the master and less willing to admit the justice of the
punishments inflicted upon them, and the right of the proprietor
to their labour.

Such was the state of things when the Act of Parliament for the
total abolition of slavery at the end of an apprenticeship of six
years came into operation. During that period the authority to
decide cases between the master and the labourer was placed in the
hands of the special magistrate. Many circumstances contributed
to render this intermediate state one productive of little satisfaction to any party, and it was by the local legislature brought
to a close two years earlier than was at first intended. It is
probable that in effect the system of apprenticeship tended to
render freedom more complete when it was ultimately obtained,
than would have been the case had the final change been more
immediate. Had the West Indies passed immediately from
slavery to freedom so soon as the master lost the authority to
inflict punishment, he would have acquired the power to dis-
miss from service. That this power would have been less
cautiously exercised, whilst the habit of punishing without
application to any legal jurisdiction continued in force, is very
probable. The necessity for referring every case, however
trifling, which required an enforcement of authority, to a magistrate, with a knowledge that all complaints on both sides
must form the subject of reports to the Governor, and also to
the home Government and the Parliament, the constant liability
to have their conduct inquired into, much more than the fines
which could be inflicted upon them, rendered the intermediate
state nearly as irksome to the white people, who had the
management of estates, as that which preceded it had been to
the labourers. To the magistrates the authority with which

they were invested was a source of peculiar hardship and annoyance. They were exposed to perpetual altercations with the planters, which were increased by their being required to visit the estates frequently. As there were no inns in many parts of Jamaica, they were compelled to be dependent on the hospitality of persons, with whom, in the discharge of their duty, they came into frequent collision. The means of supporting their families were often, under the circumstances in which they were placed, found to be inadequate. A large number of them died soon after their arrival in the West Indies. To the local legislatures the apprenticeship was an occasion for the infringement of what they maintained to be their rights, whilst it was regarded by a large class in the mother country, and also by some parties in the West Indies, as a system oppressive to the negroes. This good effect was, however, produced, that all classes were induced to consider freedom a desirable change. Not a voice was lifted against it in the House of Assembly or the Council in Jamaica—not a newspaper that did not join in the cry for immediate emancipation, which it was predicted would render the island

> " Great, glorious, and free,
> The first flower of the earth, the first gem of the sea."

On the 1st of August, 1838, when the great change was accomplished, the places of worship were crowded, impressive discourses were delivered, which partook of the enthusiasm of the occasion, and were listened to with breathless attention. The prisons were nearly emptied, from the number of pardons granted. Everything betokened a mighty revolution, the more surprising from the silence with which it was attended. What have been the effects of the change it might be important to consider.

CONCLUDING REMARKS.

THE unpublished portions of my daughter's work refer to schools; ministers; local governments; property and labour; agricultural system; industrial improvements; foreign trade and trade with the mother country; internal trade. The publication of these portions will depend on the degree of acceptance with which this may meet from its readers.

In order to show the industry, morality, and loyalty of the people in that district of Jamaica with which I was connected, having been the stipendiary magistrate from January, 1835, to July, 1841, I transcribe from a Report presented to Parliament a letter, forwarded by Lord Metcalf to the Colonial Office, with an Address from the freed labourers of St. Andrew's. I left them in 1841, with great regret, not from choice, but impelled by a sense of duty. The freed labourers of Jamaica are much further advanced in civilization and morals than those of the colonies subsequently acquired from France and Holland by conquest, and if the latter appear to be more prosperous at this moment it must be owing in some measure to the greater fertility of the soil and the financial aid afforded to them by Parliament. Jamaica is one of the finest and most improveable of our colonies, and without disrespect to his successors, of whom I really know nothing, I may venture to express the opinion, that had that most wise, philanthropic, and benevolent Governor, whom I left in the colony (Lord Metcalfe) been able to remain there, he would have found a way to destroy many of the evils of which the colonists now complain. I cannot, however, permit myself to doubt of the final well-being and prosperity of this colony in a state of freedom. It was under Lord John Russell's adminstration of the Colonial Office (by whom Lord Metcalfe was sent out) that the spirit and prospects of the people began to revive. What they now require is, a wise, experienced, and patriotic governor; some addition to the Council;

and the same financial aid as that which has been rendered to
our own landowners, and also to some other colonies, to enable
them to drain the coast-lands, and to adopt the improved
methods of manufacturing sugar. The mountainous parts (at
least half the country) are both fertile and healthy; and I
know no reason why they should not be cultivated by Europeans.
During the whole period of my residence (with a large family)
on the St. Andrew's mountains, I never found occasion to apply for the attendance of a medical man; and in proof of the
fertility of the soil I may mention the fact, that on the same
land I have grown four crops of corn in succession, without
manure; and in my garden, I grew three crops of potatoes also
in succession, on the same land and in the same year. The
plantain, banana, yam, cassava, sweet-potatoe, and arrowroot,
grow in luxuriance on the mountains, with little labour, and
I have seen beautiful canes, cotton, and coffee, growing on high
elevations. Humboldt calculates that an acre of plantains will
produce as much wholesome and nutritious food as forty-four
acres planted in Europe with potatoes, or one hundred and
thirty-three with wheat. Many small colonies of English settlers
drawing workmen at their own expense from the free labourers of
the African race, requiring employment, in the United States, or
Canada, might be formed to advantage on these mountains; and
if a few such were established, they would grow coffee, cotton, and
provisions so profitably, as to lead, ultimately, to the settlement
of thousands of European families in Jamaica, the climate of
the elevated parts of which, is justly esteemed more favourable
to health and enjoyment than even this country, by, I believe,
all who have resided there. I am sure that forced emigration, of unskilled labourers, will not be found so advantageous as that of a voluntary character. The country must
be made attractive to industrious, intelligent, skilful, and vir-
tuous families, who with a view to their own advantage, will
emigrate, and by example as well as precept, stimulate the creole
population, and help to render the whole country free and
prosperous. What has heretofore been effected by manual
labour will, in future, be accomplished far more economically
by the aid of skill, mechanism, and capital, under the direction

of such persons, and it cannot be doubted that they are neces-sary to the full development of the resources of this colony, under the new circumstances in which the spirited and bene-volent exertions of the people of the mother country have placed it. Again, I make my appeal to the admirers, friends, and descendants of Wilberforce, Clarkson, Buxton, and Gurney, to come to the aid of the colonists, and to complete the work which is yet to be done. That the courageous and noble-minded women of England, who have interested themselves on behalf of the American slaves, will be equally brave and spirited in their movements in favour of the British West India colo-nists, no one acquainted with them in the slightest degree, can for a moment doubt. The way to put an end to slavery all over the world is to make our own colonies prosperous; and just now Jamaica, and, perhaps, Antigua and Dominica, stand in most need of help.

There is an admirable passage in Mr. Douglas's book on the Advancement of Society, which well deserves the attentive con-sideration of all the friends of African freedom, both here and in America. " The principle which is ultimately destructive of slavery is this, that free labour in more valuable than the labour of slaves. In the constitution of man, fear is a deterring, but not naturally an impelling motive; it is hope alone that ani-mates and urges forward. Again, it is not the strength, but the intelligence of man, which confers its chief value on his ex-ertions; but the slave-holder is compelled to deteriorate his labour by brutallising them—for the intelligence which would make them valuable would also make them free. Thus, when-ever a fair competition arises between free and slave labour, the slave-holder must, in the end, be driven out of the market; and it is only by monopoly that the slave system can be main-tained. In those changes then, which are spreading over the globe, and which, by bringing its extremes into commercial intercourse, are about to destroy all monopolies, we possess, the true principles of enfranchisement, which will knock off every fetter, and will suffer the earth only to be productively tilled by willing hands."

S. B.

THE FREED NEGROES' SONG FOR THE 1ST OF AUGUST, 1838.

THE following song, composed by the author of the preceding pages, was sung to the tune of *Auld Lang Syne*, by tens of thousands of Negroes in Jamaica on the first day of freedom. It was printed and gratuitously circulated on the estates in St. Andrew's, Port Royal, and adjacent parishes, in anticipation of the day of freedom, and reprinted, I have heard, in England, and privately circulated, by that most benevolent and truly Christian lady, the Honourable Caroline Fox, sister of the late Lord Holland.

I.

Yes, we are free; our sunny isle,
　　Has burst the long worn chain,
And waits for Heaven's approving smile
　　To bless fair freedom's reign.

II.

Yes, we are free, for man no more
　　Claims here despotic sway,
The fetters gone, that bound before;
　　We hail the auspicious day!

III.

The day of hope, for future joy,
　　Illumes our onward way;
Slavery no more shall bliss destroy,
　　Binding the spirit's play.

IV.

The day of hope, for now we rise,
　　Unchecked by man's control,
Our Maker lives beyond the sky,
　　He only owns the soul.

V.

To Him we bow, nor man can dare,
　　Usurp the rights of Heaven,
For God must reign triumphant where
　　His choicest boon is given.

VI.

Then bloom our orange groves more sweet,
　　Our palms majestic rise,
Midst spicy shades, free spirits meet,
　　Beneath the clear blue skies.

VII.

Rise lovely island, He who came,
　　The captive souls to free,
Will watch thy progress, cause thy name,
　　To sound o'er land and sea.

VIII.

And when earth's myriads round the throne,
　　Await their final doom,
Thy sons the God of love will own,
　　Raised from the darksome tomb.

IX.

Burst every chain of death and sin,
　　Their spirits pure and free,
Earth's fetters gone, shall Heaven begin,
　　Heaven's Maker shall they see!

COPY OF A DESPATCH FROM LORD JOHN RUSSELL TO THE
RIGHT HON. SIR C. T. METCALFE, BART, G.C.B.

Downing Street, 27th September, 1839.

SIR,

IT appears to me upon considering the despatches of your predecessor, and the intelligence received by various parties in this country from Jamaica, that no improvement in legislation, and no ability in government, can secure to the island prosperity and peace unless a better spirit can be infused into the various orders of society.

I am willing to attribute the present exasperation to causes fully equal to the production of such effects; the vast nature of the change from slavery to entire freedom; the anger produced on the one side by the abridgment of the term of apprenticeship fixed by act of Parliament; and the jealousy subsisting on the other that the power of enforcing labour would be surrendered in words, but maintained in reality.

Still, whatever may be the causes, I trust that time and reflection will convince all classes that the ruin, or at least the loss and injury of all classes, must ensue from a continuance of the present animosities.

The owners and proprietors, if they cannot conciliate the negro labourers, will see the cultivation of their estates gradually abandoned, and their lands become less and less productive

The labourers, if they shall be induced to prefer the mere means of life to the wages and earnings of a comfortable subsistence, will yearly decline in civilization, become an ignorant, degraded class in society, and lose all the advantages which may be secured by a moderate degree of industry and exertion.

It will be to little purpose that the various classes by mutual crimination shall endeavour to throw the largest share of blame on each other. The island will be equally a sufferer; the friends of freedom will equally deplore; the interests of the empire will equally rue such a result.

Nor as to the blame, will any party escape the censure of an impartial world. It is extravagant to expect from the negro a degree of toil, which a white man in a similar situation would not perform, it is unjust to refuse to the employer of labour that continued exertion which can alone make it profitable to him to pay high wages.

But it is from the abuse of legal and constitutional rights, that the greatest mischiefs may be derived; if every man is to push to the utmost, privileges which are vested in him for the good of the whole, no community can remain in harmony, and a free constitution becomes a calamity, and not a blessing.

I shall have other opportunities of addressing you on the various measures which the present state of affairs may require, the purpose of this despatch is to impress most earnestly, what your own experience will have already taught you, that no change or modification of laws, will lead you successfully through your present difficulties, unless you can inculcate temper, forbearance, and charity among the Queen's subjects in Jamaica; for whose happiness and lasting welfare, without distinction of class, or colour, Her Majesty feels the most lively solicitude.

I have, &c.,

(Signed)　　　　　J. RUSSELL.

The Right Hon. Sir C. T. Metcalfe, G.C.B.
　&c.　　　　&c.　　　　&c.

COPY OF A DESPATCH SENT THROUGH THE RIGHT HON. SIR C. T. METCALFE, BART., G.C.B., TO LORD JOHN RUSSELL.

St. Andrews, Oct. 31, 1839.

MY LORD,

I HAVE the honour to forward to your Lordship an address from the lately freed labourers of this parish, which they will be very much obliged to you to present to Her Majesty.

These people have conducted themselves so admirably, and are so loyally, peacefully, and industriously inclined, that I am sure your Lordship will feel that I, who have lived in the midst of them for nearly five years; ought to do them all the service in my power; and I can do them no greater, as I think, than to accustom them to look up to their Sovereign, and the Government which enjoys, as it deserves, Her Majesty's confidence, as their assured protectors and unchanging friends.

When I state to your Lordship that at the district court I attend weekly, as stipendiary justice, offences are so rare that only one person has been sent from it, for the last six months, to prison; and that the whole amount of fines imposed during the same period has not exceeded £6 sterling;—and when I also state that a larger crop was sent to market from it this year than the last, and that there is good reason to expect a still better the next, I am sure your Lordship will feel as I do on the subject.

I have, &c,
(Signed) STEPHEN BOURNE.

To the Right Hon. Lord John Russell,
&c. &c. &c.

TO THE QUEEN'S MOST EXCELLENT MAJESTY.

May it please your Majesty,

We, your Majesty's dutiful subjects, the lately freed labourers of the parish of St. Andrew's, in public meeting assembled at the Court House, Halfway Tree, beg leave to offer to your Majesty the assurance of our loyalty to the throne; our attachment, gratitude, and entire devotion to that liberal, enlightened, and benevolent Government over which your Majesty presides; and our best wishes and constant prayers that your Majesty's reign over a free, united, and prosperous people, may be long and happy.

So far are we from entertaining the unworthy suspicion which has, as we understand, been attributed to us by those who are unacquainted with our feelings and characters, viz., that your Majesty's Government has desired to deprive us of our rights and privileges as freemen, we now most unhesitatingly declare that we repose the most entire confidence in the integrity, liberality, and benevolence of your Majesty's Government; and that it will be our anxious desire to strengthen its hands by

E

all the means in our power, because we are persuaded that its influence will be employed, as it has hitherto been, in the promotion of freedom for the African race, the union and prosperity of the British empire, and the peace and happiness of mankind. To that Government we feel ourselves indebted, under God, for our deliverance from slavery; for upright and independent magistrates; for countenance and protection afforded to our Christian instructors; for security in the enjoyment of life and liberty, and for the hopes which your Majesty's Government have, by their past exertions on our behalf, inspired, that we and our children shall be secured in the enjoyment of those blessings which have hitherto resulted from the maintenance of your Majesty's authority in this island.

We beg leave to assure your Majesty that we are by no means unwilling to pay a fair and adequate rent for the houses and grounds we occupy; that we do not refuse to labour for moderate wages; that we do not desire to live indolently, and therefore uselessly, to ourselves and others; that we are not unjust or ungrateful to those who treat us with fairness and civility; and that should an inquiry be instituted by your Majesty's desire, as to the rents we have paid and continue to pay, and the labour we have bestowed on the cultivation of sugar and coffee since we were made free, and as to the present state of the fields and provision grounds on which we have been and still are working in reference to the expected crops, it will be found that we have been greatly misrepresented by those persons who have stated, that now we are free, we have become unjust, ungrateful, or indolent.

We have laboured for others as well as for ourselves and our children; we feel it to be our duty to labour, and we shall continue so to do, in the assured hope that your Majesty's Government will secure to us the enjoyment of the fruits of labour, so that every subject of your Majesty may be enabled to " sit under his own vine and his own fruit-tree, none daring to make him afraid."

We thank your Majesty for all you have done for us: we repose entire confidence in the justice, humanity, and firmness of your Majesty's councillors; and we assure your Majesty that our daily prayers are offered up "to Him, by whom kings and queens reign, and princes decree justice," that his choicest blessings may be poured upon your head, and that your Majesty may continue—long continue—to enjoy health, prosperity, and happiness.

Signed on behalf, and by the unanimous desire of the meeting,

STEPHEN BOURNE, Justice of the Peace, Chairman.

LONDON:

G. J. PALMER, SAVOY STREET, STRAND.

SUGGESTIONS

RELATIVE TO

THE IMPROVEMENT OF THE

BRITISH WEST INDIA COLONIES,

BY MEANS OF

Instruction by Ministers of Religion and Schools.
The Relations of Property and Labour.
Agricultural and other Industrial Improvements.

&c. &c.

WITH ESPECIAL REFERENCE TO

THE INCREASED CULTIVATION OF THE SUGAR CANE
AND COTTON

IN

JAMAICA AND BRITISH GUIANA.

BY

A RESIDENT IN THE WEST INDIES FOR THIRTEEN YEARS.

WITH AN

INTRODUCTION AND CONCLUDING REMARKS

BY A LATE

STIPENDIARY MAGISTRATE IN JAMAICA.

LONDON :
THOMAS BOSWORTH, 215, REGENT STREET.
1853.

LONDON :
G. J. PALMER, SAVOY STREET, STRAND.

INTRODUCTION.

THE design of this publication cannot, I think, be misunderstood. It does not relate to the personal grievances or annoyances of which we might perhaps have some reason to complain, but to that which seems requisite to secure the establishment of freedom and prosperity to the British West India Colonies, in which we lived for above thirteen years.

I went with my family to Jamaica, in 1834, at the suggestion of the late Lord Holland, who was very anxious that the Government, of which he was so great an ornament, should succeed in their attempts to put an end to slavery everywhere, by means of a successful example in the British Colonies. His lordship was not only a true friend to the Government and the Colonies, but a warm-hearted friend of mine, and this he proved by such a degree of confidence and unreserved communication of his opinions and feelings, as could not fail to inspire esteem, and desire to deserve its continuance: not only did he give me the strongest letters of recommendation to the Marquis of Sligo, then Governor of Jamaica, and Mr. M'Neil, his own agent; but procured me letters of a similar kind from the Marquis of Normanby and the late Lord Seaford, to their friends.

To show how far we were likely to have had means of ob-

---

iv

taining accurate information, and how strong were our motives for acquiring it, I will venture to do that, to which I am sure the writer would not have objected if he were now alive. The following letter is so characteristic; so indicative of the humility, the kindness, the benevolence, the patriotism, and the practical wisdom of the noble-minded man who penned it, and sent it to me about two months after my arrival in Jamaica, that I am sure those who knew and loved him will peruse it with satisfaction.

"*February* 28*th*.

" DEAR BOURNE,

" Your letter gave me unfeigned pleasure, and I· congratulate you on being so well placed by Lord Sligo, and on the prospect which the very fair declarations of Lord Aberdeen last night held out, of an increase of salary which, I think, all parties now allow to be just and necessary. Do not on any account think of migrating with your wife and children to Savannah la Mar. As far as I am concerned, I assure you that the intelligence you are likely to collect and convey to me from the neighbourhood of Kingston is infinitely more valuable to me than anything you could do or say in Westmoreland. If you could keep Mr. M'Neil well-informed of the general views of Government, and suggest to him the best means of quietly, and in a silent way, co-operating with them, your residence in Jamaica, so advantageous I hope to the community, and agreeable I trust to yourself, will not be indifferent and unuseful to me.

" I enclose a copy of some hints I sent by this packet to Mr. M'Neil, and I have also furnished Lord Sligo with a copy. If there is anything foolish or ignorant in them, in Lord Sligo's judgment (and it is not unlikely that there may be), I hope you will advise Mr. M'Neil of it, and tell him that it is my wish to suppress any part of the paper which does not accord with the general views of Lord Sligo's government. I say this for two

v

reasons; first, because disinterested and unbiassed persons on the spot must be better judges of the practicability and expediency of such matters than I can be at this distance; and, secondly, because nothing but the co-operation of many individuals, with the assistance and sanction of the stipendiary magistracy and of Government too, can subdue the prejudices, and defeat the manœuvres of those, who in their hearts wish to bring back the whip; and therefore even a less unexceptionable effort, if concerted with the magistracy, government, and neighbourhood, is better than the most perfect one if confined to the individual estate or proprietor.

" With respect to our home politics, on which you are curious, it is, I think, quite clear that the present ministry cannot last. Our victories, as you will see by the papers, are frequent, and must, ere long, be decisive. There will, perhaps, be much greater difficulty in using, than in obtaining, the victory. You will be delighted to hear that Lord John, as leader, rises daily in parliamentary and public estimation, and in none more so than in that of Mr. Peel himself. The Dissenters will, I make no doubt, obtain all their objects. I wish I thought the poor Jews would do so too, but they are few and powerless; and the cruel, when they dare not amuse themselves by baiting a bull, console themselves by spinning a cockchafer. I see Jamaica does better, and that Mr. Bravo is a member of the Legislature. I hope he will do credit to the principle of comprehension and toleration. My sister and Mrs. Callcot are very earnest and busy about the schools in Kensington, and Mr. R. Vaughan is about to establish another. I believe the poor bill works well. Lady H. thanks you for your remembrance, and she and Allen join in best regards, and hope that Mrs. Bourne and your children (and among them a little creole) are all doing well. I am ever

"Yours,

" VASSALL HOLLAND."

The following letter, of a later date, shows clearly the views taken by the Noble Lord on the subject of education :—

"*November* 22*nd*, 1837.

" DEAR BOURNE,

"I should be very insensible indeed if I were not to acknowledge that your letter of the 13th October, and many of the statements it contained, were not only interesting, but most soothing and agreeable to me—but much as your report of what immediately affects my own interests and conscience (which perhaps your friendship led you to consider with rather too indulgent and partial an eye), I can assure you that I rejoice in no part of your letter more than in the picture of health, and comfort, and prospects of improvement of yourself and family, and the confidence you seem by your zeal to have inspired in Sir Lionel Smith. The head ploughman (I wish you had mentioned his name) shall have his high shoes, and I hope the lessons of the Education Board have long since arrived. I quite agree in thinking that education is the one thing needful—but though I also agree in the justice, expediency, and necessity of excluding no religious sect, I am, at the same time, of opinion that the main object and immediate purpose of the education should be those religious duties common to all religions, temperance, charity, honesty, and industry, and not particular, and above all, abstruse, mysterious, and disputed points of faith. I hope what you call Miss Fox's Irish education tracts will have reached their destination ere this. Lord Sligo was present at meeting of Parliament, and always speaks kindly of you. Our home politics are too long a chapter for a letter. All parties are captivated, and with reason, with our young Queen. And there is nothing which threatens to disturb the prosperity of the country, and not much, if all who really wish to preserve it, act with decent prudence and discretion, to shake the stability of Melbourne's ministry.

" Yours,

"VASSALL HOLLAND."

The Rector of St. Andrew's, the Rev. Mr. Campbell; his assistant, Mr. Pittar; the Church missionary, Mr. Cork; the Baptist missionary, Mr. Gardiner; the Presbyterian minister, Mr. Wordie; the Independent missionaries, Mr. Woolridge and his associates, and the American missionaries, whose names I have forgotten, visited us at our house in the Jamaica mountains, and with them all, the writer of the following pages entered into the freest conversation on the subjects on which she now ventures to express her opinions. The same remark applies to that most benevolent and worthy man the Archdeacon of Berbice, the late Mr. Fothergill; Mr. Seely, the Rector of New Amsterdam; the Presbyterian ministers, Mr. Stevenson and Mr. Bell; the Independent missionaries, Messrs. Ketley, Dalgleish, Davis, Waddington, and many others, with whom we had the pleasure of frequent and familiar intercourse during the six years of our residence in British Guiana; so that few persons could have better opportunities than the writer of forming a sound and impartial judgment as to the opportunities and qualifications of the instructors of the people. That able and kind-hearted man, Mr. D. O'Reilly, Attorney-General of Jamaica; the late Speaker of the House of Assembly, Mr. Dallas; the late Chief Justice of British Guiana, Mr. Bent; and the other judges, as well as Dr. Shier, and members of the Legislatures of Jamaica and Guiana favoured us with their company and correspondence on many occasions; whilst frequent intercourse with managers of estates, stipendiary magistrates, and the labouring classes who attended the Sunday-school and the courts, gave us the fullest opportunity of gaining information on the general subjects of agriculture, labour, and commerce.

I cannot therefore think that in the present state of the colonies, and considering the agitation which now prevails in the United States in relation to slavery, my daughter would have been justified in allowing any feelings of a personal nature to interfere with her desire to add her mite to the general stock of information on subjects which must ever be of deep and increasingly powerful interest to our countrymen and women until the noble experiment which England has made shall have proved so completely successful as to have caused the entire destruction of slavery all over the world. Christianity and enlightened government are wholly incompatible with slavery in any shape or of any degree. As the former *must triumph*, the latter *must be overthrown;* and it is the part of every Christian, and every friend to good government, to use his power, be it much or little, to accelerate the period when "every son of Adam shall be free."

With regard to schools, I may observe that I have been long convinced of the desirableness and importance of rendering them so far as possible self-supporting. In accordance with the suggestion of the late Lord Holland, I set to work to establish such a school near my own house at Strawberry Hill. The following announcement of my intention appeared in the *Colonial Freeman :—*

" SCHOOLS OF INDUSTRY IN JAMAICA.

" The first of these schools, an outline of the plan of which was announced in an early number of the *West Indian*, will be opened on the 1st of August, 1838, at Strawberry Hill and Brown's Cottage, in the parish of St. Andrew.

" The pupils will, in the first instance, be twenty boys, from twenty plantations in the parish of St. Andrew. They will be taught to read, write, and keep accounts; to print books for their own use and that of other schools; to cultivate the soil, in order to raise provisions and vegetables for their own consumption; to plant, clean, prune, and cure coffee, and generally to provide for their own wants, and assist their fellow-creatures. So soon as they are properly trained, they will be encouraged and assisted to become teachers of the labouring classes on the plantations to which they have been attached.

" The second school, on the same principle, will be established on Friendship Estate, the property of Lord Holland, in Westmoreland, and a third at Montpelier, in St. James's, the property of Lord Seaford.

" The necessary buildings for the school, lodging, and boarding rooms for the first establishment, will be of the plainest and cheapest kind, and erected by the apprenticed labourers belonging to various estates in the eastern district of the parish of St. Andrew.

" The custodes, magistrates, and planters, in the St. Andrew's and Port Royal Mountains, are respectfully invited to take part in the execution of this plan, which is designed to promote the true interests of the proprietors and managers of estates, as well as the labouring population.

" Any person disposed to countenance or assist in the work, may communicate with the Editor of the *Colonial Freeman*, by letter, to be left at the office in Kingston."

The only persons, however, who appeared to take an interest in it were—the late Lord Holland, the Attorney-General, Mr. and Mrs. Dallas, Mr. and Mrs. Candler, and that most estimable and noble-hearted man, the late Lord Metcalfe. The following letter from his secretary, now the Governor of the Mauritius, deserves publication as another proof of the generous and noble character of Lord Metcalfe :—

" Highgate, Oct. 7th, 1840.

" MY DEAR SIR,

" Your letter of the 14th ult. only reached me on the 1st inst., and your former one, I am ashamed to say, was mislaid.

" I am desired to return Mr. Rich's Lecture, and to request that you will keep it. His Excellency entirely approves of the objects to which the school is directed, and shall rejoice exceedingly at its success. But he did not know that it was originally intended to feed, clothe, and lodge the pupils, which

limits the advantages held out by the system of education to a
very small number of boys, by increasing so largely the expenses of each admitted into the school; but as you appear to
consider this as a necessary or expedient part of the interesting
experiment, his Excellency does not wish to offer any objection.

" The gratuitous assistance of your brother and sons in teaching the boys is most valuable, and Sir Charles is indebted to you
for it and every other part of the management of the infant institution.

" The expenses are unavoidable under the circumstances, to
which you contribute, in addition to the devotion of your time
and intellect, by supplying the premises and land, and pasture
for the packhorse.

" The lessons, as well as the elementary books, appear to the
Governor to be unobjectionable and good. I beg to return
them, and to say, that his Excellency will be happy to communicate further with you on the subject when he returns to town
for the legislative sessions.

" A cheque for £50 is herewith inclosed, which will serve
to repay your advances, and to meet any further charge that
may occur.

" I am, my dear sir,
" Yours very truly,
" J. M. HIGGINSON."

If the enlightened and truly wise policy of the noble-
minded statesmen, whose letters I have transcribed, had been
followed out ever since, how different would be the general
state of Jamaica now! That policy was to unite the good
both at home and in the colonies in the removal of everything calculated to prevent the prosperity of *all* the people; to
repress, by all possible means, the spirit of faction, exclusive-
ness, and selfishness; and to encourage and sustain every
rational effort to raise the mass by means of good government,
equal laws, and sound education. To maintain the authority

of the Sovereign, and the supremacy of the law, and to edu-
cate the young of every class, sect, and colour, in such a manner as to qualify them to be useful to each other, their families, their country, and mankind, these true statesmen
spared no labour or expense; much less did they discoun-
tenance the efforts of others who were willing to suggest or
co-operate. If Jamaica and the other West India colonies are
ever so to rise as to be examples to the slave-holding states,
this policy must be revived, and to revive it should be the
united, steady, energetic, and persevering effort of all the
friends of freedom and mankind, both in this country and the
colonies.

If we would abolish slavery in America, Brazil, and Cuba,
we must render our own colonists really and permanently prosperous. To use the significant words of Robert Hall, "We
must increase their light, and they will follow of their own
accord." It is in vain to attempt to push men beyond it.
That enlightened, benevolent, and courageous woman, Mrs.
Stowe, has done much; but it is ours to show in its com-
pleteness, a successful example of freedom in our own colonies.
This will be the best method of supporting her noble efforts.
If the ladies of England will help us, the work will soon be
done.

In a concluding chapter I propose to express my own opinions very freely, as to the means by which the Government,
Parliament, and people of England, may promote such a result.
It will be far more easy to ensure success now, than it was
first to arouse the public attention to the subject, and to induce
the people of England to make the pecuniary sacrifices they
did, to bring matters to their present position. We know
who hath said, " He who putteth his hand to the plough and
looketh back, is unfit for the kingdom of God." We dare not
withhold our energies from this noble cause until, by God's
blessing, we have made the West Indies examples to mankind.

SUGGESTIONS,

&c.

INSTRUCTION BY THE MINISTERS OF RELIGION.

HAVING endeavoured to show in a former publication* in what manner the principles of Law and Government have been affected by the changes recently introduced into the West Indies, it becomes now a matter of importance to inquire what means are to be adopted for bringing the minds of the people into conformity with the altered state of society. An attempt has been made to prove that great radical changes cannot be carried into effect without something like preparation, rendering the subjects of these changes willing to adopt them ; that where such changes result merely from the pressure of an external force they are seldom successful, and usually regarded with disapprobation, even by those whom it is intended to benefit ; but there is probably a period in the history of every country in which the community are just so far convinced of the recti- tude of certain principles as to admit that it is the duty of their rulers to enforce them, and yet too little impressed with the truth and importance of these principles to be able themselves to carry them into effect with that consistency which can alone ensure success. We may refer, as an instance, to the era of the Reformation in England. Long before Henry VIII. found

* "The British West India Colonies in connexion with Slavery, Emancipation, etc." London : Bosworth.

B

it convenient to throw off subjection to the see of Rome, Wickliffe had proclaimed some of the leading doctrines on which that Reformation was founded, and the Lollards had shown by their sufferings the sincerity of their belief in these doctrines. In this way the minds of the people had doubtless been prepared for the fundamental change in the religion of the country which was afterwards effected, so that it became both practicable and politic that a monarch whom we cannot suppose to have acted under the influence of the pure doctrines of Christianity, should declare himself and his kingdom independent of papal subjection. But had the minds of the people attained to anything like a settled conviction in regard to these important subjects, would it have been possible to re-establish Popery under Mary? would the contests between the Puritans and Episcopalians have been connected as they were with the civil wars which followed? or would the Nonconformists, who maintained the ascendency under Cromwell, have been proscribed and persecuted after the Restoration? Do not all these circumstances show, that, whilst the people asserted the right to think for themselves, they had not yet learnt to think rightly; that there was a fluctuation between opposite opinions and principles, which inflicted martyrdom on the adherents of every shade of belief, as one dogma after another attained a hold either on the minds of the people or their rulers? That vacillation which has tarnished the memory of Cranmer, may be regarded as a representation of the general uncertainty in matters of faith, which may be viewed as the natural result of imperfect information; and as the venerable archbishop became at last a witness in the flames to those great truths which had dawned on the human intellect, so the country eventually arrived at that steadfastness which has rendered her the bulwark of Protestantism, and the protector of the rights of conscience in the most distant portions of the world. That the general diffusion of truth, which could alone produce any settled convictions or consistency of conduct, should follow rather than precede a change in the established religion of the country, seems to have been a matter of necessity. So long as a deference to human authority rather than Divine was enforced by law, and generally regarded as justifiable, it was not likely that an inquiry would be made into those eternal principles on which all religion is founded. The multitude would be inclined to follow first one leader, and then another, rather as chance, or caprice, or a regard to their worldly interests directed, than from any decided preference; and it was only after an opportunity had been afforded them of examining the pretensions of all, that any rational choice could be made.

The change from slavery to freedom in the British West Indies differs chiefly from the Reformation in this, that in the one case an effort was made to ascertain what were the truths which the Almighty had seen fit to reveal to mankind, rather than what the Pope and the Roman Catholic Church required should be believed; in the other, it was maintained that human beings are called upon to perform those duties which the Almighty requires from them, rather than the actions which a master might claim from those who were subject to his control. The one was a question of faith, the other of practice. Luther promulgated the doctrine of justification by faith, but as it is admitted that if faith is a matter of such importance, it is the duty of every individual to use the utmost efforts to ascertain what is the true faith; as it is only by so doing that he can hope to attain salvation, it must be highly culpable in any ruler or teacher to exercise such an authority as may prevent the truth from being discovered or proclaimed. Every one who believed himself to be acquainted with the truth feared that he might be called on to answer for the blood of his brother if he did not make it known, and it was doubtless this strong sense of duty which led the reformers to insist on liberty of conscience for themselves, even where they did not possess the liberality to grant it to others. A further consideration of the obligations which human beings owe to their Maker tends to show that as soon as the truth is discovered it must be reduced to practice. It is by following out this rule that such wonderful improvements in machinery, in agriculture, in medicine, and in every department of civilised life have been the result of modern discoveries in science, and it is therefore to be expected that in the moral world, truth will be equally efficacious.

But how can this be the case so long as one man possesses an absolute control over the action of others ? According to the principles of slavery, the rulers may indeed be accountable to the Almighty: those whom they rule are simply accountable to them. It is not permitted that the slave should consider what is right in itself, or in conformity with the will of his Maker, but what his master requires. If we suppose the master to be perfect, he will require nothing that is opposed to the commands of the Deity, and in this case difficulties will not occur. Indeed if the master is so much better instructed than the slave that the latter does not perceive that he is ever required to do that which his conscience tells him is morally wrong, he may act with greater propriety under the control to which he is subject than he would if left to his own guidance. But as soon as he begins to understand that the will of his Creator and the will of an earthly master are sometimes at variance, dissatisfaction will ensue, a struggle between apparently conflicting claims will lead to doubt and hesitation; and further inquiry will show that what appeared at one time to be the highest duty must be sacrificed to another still more binding. This being the case, it can scarcely be doubted that the religious instruction received by the negroes in the West Indies during slavery tended to weaken the authority of the master. It may even have led many of them to imagine that they were justified in throwing off the yoke imposed upon them, innocent as the teachers of religion may have been of an intention to produce rebellion. It can scarcely be doubted that the civil wars which have taken place in most countries of Europe since the Reformation have been intimately connected with religion; and would it be surprising if similar causes had produced like effects on the opposite shores of the Atlantic ?

Many proofs might be adduced that the negroes were in the habit of comparing the authority exercised by the master with that of the Supreme Being. On one occasion, an old woman, an African, was asked whether she expected a good crop from her provision grounds. The reply was, pointing upwards, "Yes, misses, dis Massa send rain." A gentleman asked some children in Jamaica, a few days after they had become free, where they belonged to ; they must have supposed the question to be, "Who do you belong to?" a little girl replied, "Only to God now, massa." As it is, however, much less difficult to ascertain what a human being requires, than what is the will of an invisible Creator, as the dependence of a slave on the master for food, clothing, and other advantages, is much more apparent than the dependence of the whole human family on the Deity, and as the punishments inflicted by human authority are more immediate and evident to the senses than the retribution of a future state, it is clear that much more reflection is necessary, if it is expected that the influence of religion should take the place of the control of the master. Slaves are but little accustomed to reflection, and they do not acquire new habits instantly on their becoming free. To supply new motives of action in the place of those which have lost their force must be a work of time. Hence it would be almost unreasonable to expect from them that steadiness of conduct and regular industry which are necessary both as regards their own welfare and that of the countries which they inhabit, until the right means have been taken for their improvement. Nor do the masters at once accommodate themselves to their altered circumstances. They are inclined to act as if they still possessed an authority which they can no longer enforce, and to neglect those means of influence which they might still successfully employ.

It cannot be said that means have not been adopted either by the West Indians themselves, or by benevolent persons in the mother country, to supply religious instruction, so that the facilities which a state of freedom afforded might be duly improved, and that influence exerted which could alone render the great measure of emancipation successful. Places of worship have sprung up as if by enchantment. The complaint is not that the ministers of religion are too few, but that they are placed so near together as to interfere with each other's labours. Large congregations meet every Sunday, not only in the towns, but in those parts of the country where it would be impossible to collect a congregation at all unless the people were willing to resort from considerable distances for the purpose of uniting to worship the Almighty. Large sums of money are devoted to these objects by the colonial legislatures, by the people themselves in their voluntary contributions, and by benevolent persons in England. At the same time it cannot be denied that there is a very general feeling of disappointment as to the result. It may be that too much has been expected; that the seed which has been recently sown cannot spring up and bear fruit immediately, that there is reason to be satisfied at present with the willingness to receive instruction so generally manifested, and to hope and believe that the practical result will follow. It may, however, be well to consider whether there are any general causes for an apparent want of success. Without noticing at present the absence of union amongst different sects, which is unhappily so prevalent, it may be well to allude to those features which are common to all, and which probably arise from the state of society in England as compared with that in the West Indies.

In Great Britain, and indeed in all countries in which the principles of religion and morality have been made known during long periods, a separation usually takes place amongst the different classes of the community. Those who are willing to attend to the doctrines of Christianity become tolerably well acquainted with its facts, they teach them to their children from the earliest periods of infancy, and perpetually exert themselves to bring their own conduct, and that of their servants and dependants, indeed of all those over whom they possess any influence, into some measure of conformity with its requisitions. In this way a kind of moral influence springs up. A regard to character produces beneficial effects even in the absence of any better principle, and the external appearance of society presents an air of decorum, and respect for the proprieties of a well regulated community, not to be met with in countries that have been scarcely visited by the same illumination. But there is another class of individuals who, not being able to accommodate themselves to the wishes and expectations of the more religious, moral, and well-disposed, become separated to a great extent from intercourse with them. They find little satisfaction in hearing their conduct perpetually reproved and stigmatised, and therefore seldom frequent places of worship. If they are persons in indigent circumstances, they are drawn by temptations, apparently slight, into the perpetration of actual crime, and involve themselves in every species of misery and destitution. If they belong to the higher and middling classes they evince in other ways a recklessness in regard to moral obligation, which causes them to be shunned by persons of more correct conduct, whom they in return regard with few sentiments of approbation. From the prevalence of this state of things the ministers of religion acquire a habit of supposing that their congregations are composed chiefly of the former class. It is necessary to proclaim that all men are sinners, because this is a fact stated in Scripture, but when an attempt is made to point out what sins have been actually committed, the conscience seldom suggests anything more heinous than some frailties of temper, some want of compassion towards the more suffering portion of mankind, an insufficient punctuality in the performance of engagements, a too eager pursuit of mere pleasure and amusement, or a general absence of that attention to religion, in preference to worldly concerns, which its importance demands. If the latter class are noticed at all it is usually in terms of severe reprobation. It is more probable that their example will be referred to as a warning to the young and thoughtless, than that serious efforts will be made to bring about their reformation with any great hope of success. It is true that a certain class of preachers are in the habit of referring to the mercy of the Almighty, even to the most guilty, in the hope of reclaiming those who are regarded as the lost and abandoned, the very outcasts of society—but the greater number consider that it is with those whose outward conduct is at least moral and decorous that they chiefly have to do; and that it is these who may be expected to pay the greatest attention to their instructions. Now, in the West Indies, it can scarcely be said that either of these two classes exist. The means of religious instruction were until lately very inefficient. Indeed, in some parts of the West Indies they scarcely existed at all. The effect of slavery, even on the white people, is to prevent that freedom of thought which is favourable to a general diffusion of information, and still more so to a habit of reasoning on subjects connected with morals and religion. The tendency of such reasonings would have been to overturn the whole social system. They were, therefore, discouraged just in proportion to the impression entertained by the masters or other persons in authority that their interests were identified with the perpetuation of that state of things which they could not but feel to be rapidly passing away. Wherever the negroes were regarded as moral and intellectual beings rather than as property, a certain degree of encouragement was given to the ministers of religion of every class. Since emancipation the number of these ministers has increased in a manner perfectly astonishing. There is one district, from which, less than fifty years ago, children were taken to England to be baptized, where it was necessary, within about thirty years, to wait two years before that rite could be performed by a clergyman of the Church of England, but where now there are upwards of twenty places of worship, most of them regularly supplied with ministers of various denominations. It is probable that there may be about a hundred black people who can read the Scriptures in many places where but one could do so ten years ago, and the circulation of the sacred writings has increased in the same proportion. But as the change has so recently taken place, the character of a great proportion of the community of every class has been formed under the influence of the former state of things, and the younger members of society have been influenced at least as much by their example as by any instruction they have received. The consequence is, that there are very few who have not participated more or less in the faults that have been generally prevalent. At the same time there has not existed that separation between the different classes of society which has the effect of leaving persons of the worst disposition to follow out their evil courses without any influence from those who are in some degree better disposed than themselves. Amongst the black people a want of moral principle appears to be chiefly the result of ignorance, amongst the white of the unfavourable circumstances in which they have been placed. In both there is much that indicates a tendency to something better than their conduct would lead strangers to expect from them. In addition to these two, there is a class of educated persons of colour from whom there is much reason to hope for improvement. But the ministers of religion have adopted a certain mode of addressing their hearers, in conformity with the characters of most of the inhabitants of the mother country, and they continue the same from habit in the West Indies. Those who having framed their sermons on the most approved models, have consulted the volumes of theology which their libraries contain, cannot suppose that the course they adopt is not the right one, and may be inclined to attribute any want of success to a determination to persevere in wrong courses on the part of their hearers. As they have been accustomed to associate with persons whose general character is deserving of respect, and as their habits and education lead them to regard every departure from right principle or practice with strong feelings of disapprobation, they find little to commend in the prevailing tone of society in the West Indies. The style of preaching they adopt is strongly tinctured with feelings of this nature. They often overlook the disadvantages which a large proportion of their hearers have experienced, and judge them as severely as they would do, had they spent their lives under the most favourable circumstances. Those who find themselves addressed in this manner must either believe that these animadversions are really justified by their own conduct, or they must conclude that the preacher is uncharitable, and disposed to condemn without necessity. In the latter case they often discontinue their attendance, or if they do listen to the discourses it is with little advantage to themselves; in the former the hope of amendment is often extinguished, rather than efforts excited such as may produce reformation. To point out the evils which exist in society is undoubtedly necessary, but there is little prospect that a good effect will result, unless a remedy is at the same time made known. The Scriptures do both; and it is according to the degree in which the ministers of religion follow the example thus set before them, that there is reason to expect their efforts will be successful. There is little doubt that when Christianity was first promulgated, there was at least as much to censure, as there can be at the present day in the West Indies, but we find that all possible encouragement was held out to those who were willing to abandon what was wrong and return to a right course. Indeed, it is expressly said, that "the Son of Man came not to call the righteous, but sinners to repentance."

There is another circumstance which affects chiefly the more ignorant classes. It is common in England, and perhaps to a still greater extent in Scotland, to suppose that those persons who are in the habit of attending to religion at all, possess at least a moderate degree of acquaintance with the narrative portions of Scripture, and those facts which are the basis of the doctrines of Christianity. This being the case, a constant repetition of these facts would be unnecessary. The consequence is that those discourses which are often most highly approved, contain chiefly reasonings on the more abstract doctrines of revelation, and sometimes these reasonings are of a character highly metaphysical. But to the greater part of the population of the West Indies discourses of this kind must be altogether unintelligible from the want of that preliminary knowledge on which they are founded, and still more so to those who possess a very imperfect acquaintance with the English language. This is particularly the case in British Guiana. The older negroes speak almost invariably what is termed the Creole Dutch, and the vocabulary of those who call themselves English, having been recently acquired, is usually very limited. Even in Jamaica and other places that have been long in the possession of Great Britain, the forms of expression, as well as the pronunciation, common amongst the people, is so different to that employed by any class of persons in the mother country, that it is extremely difficult for those who are unaccustomed to their phraseology either to understand their meaning or make themselves understood when they have occasion to give them the plainest directions. It is not surprising that a hindrance should thus present itself to their obtaining information either from reading the Scriptures themselves, or in listening to the instructions delivered to them. Difficulties of this kind do not so much arise from a want of intelligence on their own part as from a want of acquaintance with the grammatical construction of the language. An individual was asked, after reading that Jesus had been born in Bethlehem of Judea, where Bethlehem was? The reply was, in heaven. Another supposed that Christ had not been put to death by Herod, along with the other children, because He was a spirit. Another was asked, after reading that Christ passed through Samaria, what was meant by Samaria? The reply was that it was the name of a woman. In these cases the mistake often arises from the circumstance that the small words, such as *of, by, for, through,* not being used in the same sense by the people themselves, are apt to be entirely overlooked. They would not say a woman of Samaria, if wishing to indicate that a person was a native of a particular country, but a Samaria woman. Where it was said a woman of Samaria, it would probably be understood to mean the woman Samaria. Of course such a mistake would render other passages where Samaria was spoken of as a place quite unintelligible. The same people will explain other passages in their own language with great readiness, as in one instance it was asked, why it was difficult for a rich man to enter into the kingdom of heaven. The answer was, " Because when he got his money, he think nobody like him." The sentence, " Bless the Lord, oh, my soul, and forget not all his benefits," was interpreted, " All the good what He do to people." In other cases they show that they understand what they are reading by substituting a word with which they are familiar for one to which they are not accustomed, without destroying the sense, as " Put up thy sword into its sheath" was read " Put up thy sword into its case ;" " Esau lifted up his voice and wept," " Esau lifted up his voice and cried." Under these circumstances it is nearly impossible to explain abstract doctrines, because they cannot be expressed in language which they are in the habit of using themselves. The ideas that are conveyed by such words as repentance or faith, &c., can scarcely be translated into the language of ordinary life, but instances may be pointed out of the manner in which these dispositions were exemplified, as in the case of the prodigal son, or of Abraham leaving his native country at the command of the Almighty. Such narratives may be easily rendered into language with which they are familiar, and that without adopting their uncouth modes of expression.

It is not merely the facts related in Scripture with which it is desirable that they should be made acquainted, with a view to their religious improvement. There are many discoveries in astronomy and other sciences, tending to show the greatness and power of the Almighty, in regard to which it would not be at all difficult to give them information, and which could scarcely fail of exciting their attention. The histories of good men in every age and country, particularly of those whose circumstances in any degree resemble their own, would present examples for their imitation, whilst instances of the evils which individuals and nations have brought upon themselves by misconduct would serve as a warning to deter them from adopting similar courses.

Another difficulty experienced by the ministers of religion, and one of which many of them complain is, that it is nearly impossible to preach in a style adapted equally to their white and black hearers. Those familiar illustrations, and explanations of the meaning of words that are suited to the comprehension of the latter class, are usually unacceptable to the former. The consequence is that in the larger towns, separate congregations are formed, and although there is, to a certain extent, a mixture of colour and of class, probably sufficient to prevent the sermon from being entirely unsuited to either, there are some places of worship, chiefly those in which the missionaries preach, where it is extremely rare for a white person to be seen. In the country districts, the black people being the most numerous, are often addressed almost exclusively, whilst the white inhabitants not unfrequently absent themselves altogether. In Jamaica, and perhaps in some other places amongst the more respectable families, it has not been unusual to carry on some kind of religious service at home, but where this is not the case the idea sometimes entertained, that it is quite unnecessary for a white person to attend any place of worship, cannot but have an injurious effect on the moral and religious feelings of the community.

Under all these disadvantages it cannot be doubted that numbers of the ministers of religion are zealously and faithfully exerting themselves to bring about a general improvement. The chief difficulty arises from the circumstances in which they have been placed having been so different to those which exist in the West Indies, that it is nearly impossible that they should at once alter their habits of thought, so as to obtain that kind of influence which it is most desirable they should exercise.

A review of this subject would be incomplete without a reference to the fact that there is scarcely a denomination of professing Christians that has not sent its emissaries to assist in the work of improving the state of things in the West Indies. Sometimes, as in Jamaica, nearly all classes are to be met with in a single locality. The Jews are also numerous in that island, and carry on their religious worship, whilst they exercise as great an influence, and enjoy as many privileges perhaps, as in any part of the world. In the smaller islands one or two sects have obtained the predominance, so as to render the interference of others in so limited a field quite unnecessary. It may be said that religious intolerance, if by this we mean such an attachment to one particular form of worship as tends to produce uncharitable feelings towards others, is by no means a prevailing feature in West Indian society. The evil is rather that of indifference or want of information, than of bigotry. It is true that some classes of missionaries have met with considerable opposition, but it has generally been on account of their opinions on such subjects as slavery or civil government, rather than from any dislike entertained in regard to their religious tenets. They might have preached any doctrines which they thought proper, had there not been a desire either on their own part or on that of their congregations that they might be reduced to practice in a way that interfered with the interests of others. It was not the truth or falsehood of these doctrines that was made the subject of inquiry, but the effect which the conduct produced by them, might have upon the state of society. Now there is little doubt that religious opinions are connected with a certain course of action which may be either injurious or beneficial to the worldly interests of a community. We find that during the civil wars in England the Episcopalians, the Presbyterians, the Independents, the Anabaptists, and the Quakers, all had their separate opinions in matters relating to the government of the country, and the same has been the case in the West Indies. It is these opinions that have occasioned the difficulties to which they have been exposed, and not their views in regard to the more spiritual part of religion. The two former classes have both proceeded on the principle that it was lawful to enforce religion without waiting for the consent of the people. They have adopted a system founded on the supposition that the clergy, the heads and rulers of the Church, were already in possession of the truth, and that it was the duty of the people generally to submit to their authority. The difference between them appears to have been this, that the Episcopalians were inclined to require a general submission to one head, whilst the Presbyterians maintained a great degree of equality amongst the ministers and elders, to which, however, the people generally were not to be admitted. It is not likely that either of these classes would encourage anything like a want of due subjection to authority of any kind amongst a people so ignorant as the negroes in the West Indies. Whatever reason they might have for maintaining their peculiar opinions in the mother country, these reasons would operate more strongly where the people were still less capable of regulating their own conduct. There is no doubt that sincere Christians of every class would endeavour to promote a system of mildness and justice rather than one of oppression and tyranny, but where it is considered that force in any case is justifiable, it is difficult to point out the precise limits within which the exercise of that force should be confined. It is probable that the most humane and benevolent individuals of these two classes would rather endeavour to prevail on the people to conciliate those who possessed authority over them by submission, than to assert any rights of their own. The Wesleyans and Moravians also joined in pursuing the same course, and have, therefore, been able to gain a footing in slave countries without exciting much hostility on the part of the planters, or giving much annoyance to the Government.

The Independents have probably met with greater difficulties in carrying out their opinions, and acquiring an influence in the West Indies than any other class. Maintaining that all authority, at least in matters of religion, depended on the choice of the people, they could not fail to entertain a decided aversion to the system of slavery, which did not permit of the exercise of this choice in matters civil or religious. At the same time, the strictness of the moral discipline which they have endeavoured to introduce has rather dissatisfied the negroes, and prevented them from obtaining the support of numbers where they were exposed to a competition with other sects who have permitted a greater latitude. In British Guiana, where they were nearly the first to occupy the field, they have succeeded in collecting together large congregations, chapels have been built in a very superior style, and they have been remarkably successful in promoting the intelligence and civilization of the people; but in addition to their disapprobation of slavery, they have been constantly desirous of a change in the general system of Government, and these circumstances have drawn down upon them the hostility of several classes of the white inhabitants. This feeling appears, however, to be gradually diminishing.

The Baptists have obtained a very extensive influence over the minds of the black people in Jamaica, who have regarded them as much in the light of defenders from temporal oppression as in that of instructors in religion.

The question as to how the ministers of religion should be supported has engaged much attention in the West Indies. This also has been more or less connected with the all-engrossing topic of freedom or slavery. The voluntary system has been supposed by its most devoted adherents to be the only one consistent with perfect religious liberty. Indeed it would appear that in this point as well as in many others, the difficulty is not to determine which principle is right in the abstract, but in what way principles that are admitted to be generally right, admit of application to particular instances. To maintain that force should be exercised in no case whatever would be to do away with all law and government. It would inflict martyrdom on the good, by leaving the bad to the government of their own lawless inclinations. At the same time it is far more desirable that people should do what is right as the result of their own convictions than from the influence of any external force. Religion as an affair between the creature and the Creator must be voluntary, that is, it cannot be subject to any human control. It is only the outward forms of religion that can be supported by any degree of force or coercion. How far these may contribute to produce the spirit which might otherwise be wanting is a fair subject for inquiry. It has also been doubted whether the plan which prevails to a considerable extent in the West Indies, of the State supporting different forms of religion, is justifiable.

In British Guiana, where everything appears to emanate from the Government, and nothing to depend on the choice of the people, the country is divided into different parishes, part of which are regarded as belonging to the Church of England, and part to the Church of Scotland. There is little doubt that this is a fruitful source of discord. Persons removing from one parish to another can scarcely change their religion in consequence, and wish to be accommodated with their own form of worship. The clergy of the Church of England are particularly desirous of propagating what they believe to be the truth, and procure grants for the erection of chapels in parishes which have been allotted to the Church of Scotland, the clergy of which, as well as the missionaries are inclined to regard them as intruders.

In Jamaica it is chiefly the English Church which is supported by the Government, but other congregations, not excepting Jews, receive grants from the House of Assembly. The tendency of things in that island appears to be to consider that the people choose their own religion, but that when they require assistance in carrying on their own form of worship, they can receive it from the revenues of the country, if they think proper to make an application for it. This may be at least consistent, and throws the responsibility of ascertaining what is truth on the teachers of religion or their hearers; but it is difficult to understand how more than one religion can be established by a Government, unless in compliance with the wishes of the people.

Notwithstanding all the difficulties that arise from these various causes, perhaps there is more reason to be surprised that so much has already been done, than that so much yet remains to do. Even where there has not been that decided effect upon the character of the population that might be desired, civilisation has been promoted, the faculties called into exercise, and the creation of new wants has been a stimulus to industry. A better class of motives has not entirely supplied the want of those which were in exercise during slavery, but there is great reason to hope that the time is not far distant when they will be more than sufficient to do so. We can scarcely suppose that those benevolent persons in England who have contributed so largely to promote improvements of this nature will withdraw their assistance until they can feel assured that it is no longer necessary, and the West Indies in that situation that they can be expected to rise as the result of the industry, the skill, the enterprise, and the moral and religious improvement of their own inhabitants.

INSTRUCTION IN THE SCHOOLS.

IT has been already stated that the efforts of the ministers of religion are by no means so successful as they might be if the acquaintance of the people with the English language, their general information, and habits of reflection, were such as to enable them fully to comprehend the instructions they receive. For the present, and as regards the older people, the only means of remedying the evil seems to be that the ministers should accommodate themselves to their capacities as much as possible. Another course, although by no means an effectual one, is frequently adopted. Black people are employed either to interpret the discourses of the white ministers, or to communicate instruction themselves in the best way they are capable of doing. It is possible that some, who could not obtain any acquaintance with the truths which it is desirable to communicate to them, unless this course were adopted, thus receive some degree of improvement. But the teachers not being very far in advance of those whom they have to instruct, probably communicate in some instances as much error as truth. Many of the wrong impressions which the people thus receive have been attributed to the missionaries. They are rather the constructions placed by these persons on the doctrines inculcated by these missionaries. Any one acquainted with the singular ideas which circulate amongst the people, the mixture of African superstitions with the superior truths of Christianity which they constantly evince, would scarcely be surprised at the errors which Protestants have so severely censured in the Roman Catholic Church, nor would they attribute these errors altogether to a design on the part of the priests to deceive the people. Such designs are often attributed to the teachers of religion in the present day in the West Indies. The impossibility of at once changing the character, the habits, and ideas of large masses is overlooked. It is presumed that the ministers of religion have an almost unlimited command over the conduct of the people, that they could at once persuade them to adopt that regular industry which both the interests of their employers and the welfare of the countries they inhabit demand from them, and that a few years of instruction might correct faults which have been the growth of centuries, indeed which have existed so long that we have no history of their commencement or their origin. Civilization and improvement have been progressing in the more northern states of Europe for nearly two thousand years. During the greater part of this time an acquaintance with Christianity has been enjoyed. We cannot suppose that the methods adopted for the propagation of this beneficent religion by its divine Founder were not the wisest and the most fitted to produce the desired end that could have been adopted ; and yet how slow has been the advance from a state of complete barbarism to that which exists at present. It is little more than three centuries since the new world was first discovered, or the Africans brought into communication with the civilised countries of Europe, and yet, during that time what changes have taken place ! A whole race has been nearly swept away, and their territory occupied by the inhabitants of the tropical or northern regions of the western world. Paths have been cut through those rocky defiles, and over those lofty and precipitous steeps of Jamaica which might almost have been supposed inaccessible. The voyager, who, having descried the bold outlines of the blue mountains rising amongst the clouds in the distance, has beheld them assume, on a nearer approach, an aspect of sunshine and verdure, finds with astonishment that on heights which at first appeared fitted only to be the abodes of the eagle and the vulture, habitations have been erected which command the most magnificent prospects, and are rendered commodious by the various advantages afforded by an improved state of society ; whilst the European rose, the mango of India, the coffee of Arabia, and the bread-fruit of Polynesia, vie with the native pimento, or the cedar, in adorning these elevated spots, and supplying the wants, or gratifying the tastes, of their inhabitants. In British Guiana an extended line of coast has been rendered susceptible of cultivation only by embankments which have been necessary to prevent the waves of the Atlantic from inundating the country to a great distance inland on the rise of the tide. Districts of this character have been intersected with canals in every direction, which were required to drain off the superfluous waters of the interior; whilst the steam-engine, the church or the chapel, and the school-house, afford facilities for supplying alike the physical and intellectual necessities of those who are located on the soil which has thus been rendered habitable. Surely it cannot be said that the West Indians have done nothing, or that their work is destined to be blotted out from the records of existence, and to leave no trace of its effects upon the happiness of the human species. The remains of multitudes of their former inhabitants of every colour and class, whose lives have been probably shortened by the arduous labours in which they have been engaged, and the physical obstacles which they were required to overcome, slumber at this moment beneath their soil, and when so much has been already accomplished, shall the fruits of their toils, their anxieties, and their sufferings, be lost for want of those exertions which are yet necessary for the accomplishment of objects which have called forth so great an amount of effort, not only in these western possessions, but amongst the inhabitants of the mother country ?

It is of the greatest importance, then, to inquire what are the best means of ensuring the fulfilment of those designs which the wise and good have entertained in regard to the West Indian possessions of Great Britain. Had the inhabitants of these countries been totally destitute of energy so much would not already have been done. Great Britain would not have been supplied with so large an amount of sugar, coffee, and other productions, whilst the people themselves obtained the means of subsistence and rendered portions of the earth which had been destitute of those improvements that are necessary to the existence of civilization, in so great a degree fitted as they are at present, to be the abodes of intellectual beings, and the scene of the comforts, the conveniences, and even the refinements requisite to render life the source of at least a certain degree of satisfaction and enjoyment. The means for calling into exercise the activity and industry of the people have no doubt been objectionable, but had there not been a capacity for exertions tending to produce these beneficial effects, no means could have been efficacious. The object is now to provide other means that will not be injurious or oppressive to any class, or inflict greater hardships than are the necessary portion of human beings, in this state of imperfection, and of liability to suffering and toil. These means, we may affirm, must be such as have a tendency to act on the moral and intellectual faculties of our nature, and to elevate rather than to degrade the characters of those upon whom they are exercised. We have already seen that religion has been regarded as one of the most powerful, and that great efforts have been made for extending its influence. But for the promotion of religion itself, as well for the furtherance of every other species of improvement, it cannot be doubted that general efforts should be made for enlarging the mental capacity, as far as it is in the power of human beings to do so. To this effect it is absolutely essential that a right direction should be given to the minds of the young, and that they should be trained in habits which are likely to render them both happy themselves and useful members of society.

Before endeavouring to point out what may be yet necessary for promoting the work of education, it may be well to consider what has been already accomplished. On the passing of the Act of Parliament for the abolition of slavery, the British and Foreign Bible Society, with most commendable liberality, resolved on presenting a copy of the New Testament and Psalms, bound together in one volume, to every emancipated negro who had learnt to read. Copies of the Scriptures were accordingly sent to every considerable town of the British West Indies, but for some time it was found that the demand by no means equalled the supply, and that numbers of those who applied for these copies read so imperfectly, that they could not be regarded as entitled to receive the valuable present which had been intended for them. There is little doubt, however, that the reception of the sacred writings by some, as a gift from their friends in England, and a token of the approbation with which their efforts in learning to read were regarded, and the hope that it might be obtained on the part of others, greatly stimulated their exertions. For some time the wants of the people were thus supplied without any cost to themselves. The demand, however, greatly increased. The people were found eager to purchase, and in one year after complete emancipation had taken place, it appears from the published reports of the British and Foreign Bible Society, that the number distributed by that Society alone in Jamaica was about one to every ten of the population. It could scarcely be supposed that the circulation could proceed in an equal proportion, as those who had once purchased would not require a fresh supply immediately. It is stated that in 1845, 5,025 copies were forwarded to that island. It is not improbable that an equal number may have been obtained from other sources. Although the diffusion of knowledge in every other part of the West Indies is not equal to that which prevails in Jamaica, the state of things generally is not very dissimilar. Trinidad is represented as being one of those places in which the least has been done for the improvement of the people. It is not to be supposed, however, that every individual who purchases a copy of the Scriptures can read with anything like ease and correctness. Those who are too old to go to school often succeed in learning their letters from some child or neighbour. They then spell over a single chapter, until they have learnt it by heart, and fatigued with so great an exertion, probably do not proceed farther for some time to come. At other times they persevere in this way until they have learnt to read without much difficulty. An elderly woman, who was unacquainted with the alphabet but a few months previously, has been known to read the first eight chapters Matthew correctly, although in any other part of the Scriptures she found it necessary to spell words of three or four letters. It was found that nearly all the people from one estate in Jamaica, about the commencement of the apprenticeship, could repeat the alphabet, and many of them spell small words, but that they could scarcely tell one letter from another unless in the regular order. On being asked who was their teacher, they replied, " Schoolmassa John Archer." Some time after, Schoolmassa John Archer requested instruction. He was an elderly black man, of mild and agreeable manners, and wore spectacles. It was found that he could read but few words of one syllable without spelling, and complained frequently at the conclusion of the sentence, that the lesson was " very heavy." On being asked what he could read, he replied, " The Prayer-book and the Wesleyan hymn-book." It is probable that he had learnt portions of these by heart. It may be mentioned as an instance of the progress of improvement, that John Archer's son and his wife, about six years afterwards, both read correctly and wrote tolerably well. An intelligent black man in Berbice remarked on one occasion, that the reason why the people did not learn was that, in former times, as soon as any one could read the first chapter of John, he was made a teacher. According to a census of the population recently taken in Jamaica, the ministers of religion are 267, that is one to rather less than 1,500 people, and the teachers 649, or one to about 600. It is probable that in connexion with most of the places of worship throughout the West Indies, there is a school the master of which is either a white, a coloured, or a black man, who has received a fair measure of instruction, and where these schools are carefully superintended by the minister, they are perhaps as efficient as it would be reasonable to expect in the present circumstances of the West Indies. In other cases great improvement is required.

Little doubt can be entertained that the progress of education, so far as learning to read and write is concerned, has been on the whole highly satisfactory. We may suppose that before very many years have elapsed the great majority of the people may, without any remarkable increase in the means of instruction, obtain as much of this kind of knowledge as would usually be expected from labouring people in England; but important differences of opinion prevail as to the effect which education has produced on the character and habits of the people. Complaints are made even by persons of intelligence, that by continuing too long at school the time is lost during which young people might be expected to acquire habits of industry, and that they are afterwards less willing to perform the labour required on estates, than they would have been, had their attention been less given to mental improvement. It is also stated by missionaries and other persons, whose exertions in promoting education render it impossible to charge them with a desire to perpetuate ignorance, that those who have been trained in the schools in a great number of instances disappoint the expectations of their friends by a want of that correctness of conduct and attention to religion which it might have been supposed that the instruction they have received would have produced. Now it is impossible to state with anything like certainty what has been the effect of education, unless we could ascertain what would have been the state of things if the degree of instruction imparted had been withheld. It is admitted that evils have accompanied the change from slavery to freedom, which those who advocated that change would seldom allow themselves to anticipate. But there is every reason to think that these evils would have been far greater if the correcting influence of moral and religious restraint, which scarcely any one will deny that education has a tendency to produce, had not been exerted. Some of the evils that are complained of prevailed long previously, and it cannot be said that they have been increased by education, but merely that education has not as yet entirely succeeded in preventing them. Others arise from the circumstance that people who have hitherto been unaccustomed to direct their own conduct, have not immediately acquired that discretion, forethought, and steadiness which were peculiarly demanded by their altered situations. There are, probably, many things which nothing but experience can teach them; and it is not surprising that the old, who chance to be at the same time the uneducated, possess this experience in a greater degree than their children, notwithstanding that the latter are able to read and write.

At the same time the character of the instruction given is of the utmost importance. The question has often been raised, whether it is better to neglect the younger portion of the community altogether, or to run the risk of communicating error. Now, in a country where the truth is generally made known, most of the systems of instruction adopted contain much more of truth than of error, and their tendency is therefore likely to be on the whole beneficial rather than injurious; but in referring to the state of those countries that have not been visited by Christianity, there is much that might lead an observer to conclude, that no education at all is better than an education based on falsehood. The Hindoos are unquestionably a more intellectual, a more civilised, and altogether a more educated people than the African negroes. Many of those who visit the West Indies as labourers can read and write their own language. In the arts of life they evince a greater degree of dexterity; and yet on estates the Africans are almost universally preferred. It is even said that one

African will do as much work as two or three Coolies. The former readily acquire, at least, an imperfect acquaintance with the English language. They imitate the dress and habits of Europeans, attend schools and places of worship, and in every respect rapidly improve. The latter retain their own habits and language, their own superstitious observances, and as yet appear little altered by any opportunities of instruction which the West Indies may afford. In Jamaica the greatest apprehensions have been entertained as to the effect of their influence on the morals of the people of the country; and it is probably from considerations of this kind, as much as because their introduction is found to be too expensive, that the House of Assembly of that island were desirous that it should be discontinued. Were missionaries alone to make such objections it would not be very extraordinary, but that any reasons of this character should influence a West Indian Legislature, unless they were in some degree justified by facts, seems very improbable, especially as there is not the same disposition to discontinue African immigration. In China, another civilised country, and one in which education is by no means neglected, a missionary, the late Dr. Morrison, as able and as zealous as it would be possible to meet with, laboured for twenty-seven years, and yet it would appear that very few conversions were effected; whilst in those countries where a written language is not to be found, and where the people appear to be immersed in the greatest ignorance and barbarism, a general profession of Christianity speedily follows its introduction, and there is at least a willingness to attend to the means of instruction. Even in Europe, we find that those nations which at the time of the promulgation of the Christian faith had been the least influenced by Greek and Roman civilisation have generally embraced the Protestant religion, and appear to have adopted a more spiritual form of worship, than those who, having been previously, to a great extent, enlightened, did not so readily relinquish their preconceived opinions even when they interfered with the doctrines of a purer faith.

Admitting, then, that the great object of education should be to communicate truth, it is necessary to consider how this can most certainly be effected. In what manner are truths in science and in every department of literature elicited ? Is it that one person, or any number of persons possessing authority, prescribe to authors what studies they shall pursue, or what they shall make known, or is it by leaving them to make their own discoveries, to follow out their own experiments, and honestly to state to others what has been the result of their investigations ? In courts of justice, where the object is to ascertain what are the real facts of the case to be determined, are not the witnesses left to make their own statements without dictation from others ? But it may be said that ignorant persons, and especially children, are incapable of judging of the truth or falsehood of what is communicated to them, and that it is therefore necessary that a supervision should be exercised in regard to the teachers, to prevent their being misled by those who are either designing, or inclined to teach what is erroneous from a want of information on their own part. There is no doubt that on this point there may be danger, but the remedy seems to be to procure as great a number of really well-instructed teachers as possible, whose moral character is at the same time without reproach, rather than to impose restrictions which can never give integrity to the dishonest, or ability and information to the incapable. There is little doubt that where truth and falsehood are fairly brought into competition, truth will ultimately prevail; but falsehood may for a long time retain an influence where nothing is done to disseminate truth.

It is stated that in Jamaica a plan has been adopted for attaining this object with the support of the Legislature ; that pupils are to be received between the ages of sixteen and nineteen, on the recommendation of the various ministers of religion, with a view to their afterwards becoming teachers ; that it is proposed to devote five days of the week to their instruction in natural philosophy, history, mensuration, algebra, grammar, composition, &c. ; that Saturdays and Sundays are to be appropriated to their religious instruction, which they may receive either from the master of the school, or from the minister of religion whom they or their parents may prefer; and

27

also that it is expected they should attend some place of worship according to the denomination to which they belong. The importance of training a class of native teachers has also engaged the attention of missionary societies, some of whom have institutions for this purpose in different parts of the West Indies. On the success of such efforts much of the prosperity of these colonies depends. It is not likely that with so scattered a population as it is usual to meet with, European teachers can be supported in sufficient numbers to supply the wants of the community. Black people can live at far less expense. Whether they are well trained or not, it is almost certain that they will be the teachers in a great many instances. The more enlarged the plan of education adopted, if it is only carried out with vigour and efficiency, the greater the prospect of its being successful, and of real utility to the countries which it is designed to benefit. In British Guiana there is an institution for the education of the native population under the superintendence of the Government and the Bishop, and a salary has also been granted for an inspector of schools. Indeed, everywhere the question does not appear to be whether education should be promotod or not, but according to what principles it should be conducted.*

Much attention has been given to the practicability of establishing schools of industry, especially in Jamaica, and efforts have been made to carry some plan of this kind into effect. A prize was offered by Lord Elgin for the best essay on the subject. Suggestions have since been sent out by the Government as to the most effectual means of promoting the object. The Baptist missionaries have stated, however, as an objection to the plan, that the people are sufficiently desirous of bringing up their children in habits of industry, on account of the advantage they derive from their labour in the provision grounds ; that they are sometimes unwilling on this account to send them to school at all, and would be still more so if they were to be required to work for others. It is probable that this would be the case, if the pupils were only employed in such simple operations as hoeing or planting the more common

* See note at p. 67.

productions of the West Indies ; indeed in such labour as they might easily learn to perform without any particular instruction. But there is a very great want of persons who can exercise any thing like skill or ingenuity, and as the parents by allowing their children to become habituated to occupations of this kind, would only render their labour afterwards the more valuable, there is little doubt that they would see the advantage to themselves of such a training. If anything like compulsion were adopted, they would imagine that the system so nearly resembled slavery that a spirit of resistance would probably be aroused, which would render any subsequent efforts unsuccessful. Before the people became free, the masters, having an interest of property in them, by teaching them any useful arts enhanced their value; but they cannot have the same inducement from self-interest to adopt this course, when those whom they have instructed can leave them at any moment. The parents would also, it is probable, object to making their children apprentices for a term of years, as is done in England, to any experienced artizan.

If any plan could be adopted according to which the mental improvement of young persons could be properly attended to, whilst they were acquiring some useful mechanical art, it would tend to remove many of the evils which are so constantly a subject of complaint. The great difficulty appears to be the expense which would be necessary in the first instance, although afterwards the value attached to labour in the West Indies might render such schools, at least to a certain extent, self-supporting. There are also few persons to be met with who possess the requisite qualifications for carrying into effect undertakings of this character. If schools of industry could not be adopted it would be desirable that advantage should be taken of any leisure time the people may possess without neglecting their ordinary occupations, to communicate to them as much instruction as possible.

It is of the utmost importance that after the period at which it is necessary that they should begin to labour for their own support, some influence should be exercised over their minds by persons of greater intelligence and more settled principles than themselves. There is great reason to think that it is for want of this influence, that their early education often turns out to be less effectual in preventing misconduct, than their friends, their teachers, and the ministers of religion could desire.

THE RELATIONS OF PROPERTY AND LABOUR.

Amongst those inherent dispositions which the Creator has seen fit to communicate to his creatures, one of the most conspicuous, and one which produces some of the most important effects on the general condition of society, is a desire to possess property. Even the child evinces a *desire* for play-things which it can call its own. The most uncivilized human being requires a hut or a canoe : but it is when an exercise of the intellectual faculties, and habits of reflection and forethought have produced a tendency to enter into enlarged calculations in regard to the future, and to objects which, from their distance and their incapacity to affect the senses, make little impression on the uncultivated mind, that this disposition becomes most strongly manifested. Christianity, so far from repressing an occupation of the mind in regard to the distant and the future, points to a far more distant country in which an inheritance is promised, and secures the possession of this inheritance through periods of eternal existence. The young man who was required to relinquish his worldly goods, and to follow the Saviour of mankind, who we are told had not a place on which to lay His head, was not commanded to do so without the hope of receiving an equivalent. He was told that he should have treasure in Heaven. The divine law which recognizes a desire for the acquisition of property also guards these rights from invasion. " Thou shalt not steal," was one of the commandments uttered from Mount Sinai ; and " Cursed be he that removeth his neighbour's landmark," was one of the denunciations to which the whole people of Israel were required to say —Amen.

The nature of property, however, varies widely in different countries, and according to the influence of circumstances. In an advanced state of civilization, and in territories that are occupied by a redundant population, where the soil is already appropriated, and for the most part covered with improvements that have been made during the possession of its successive owners, property in land is that to which the greatest importance has been attached. But in uncivilized and comparatively uninhabited countries, the case is widely different. Europeans have usually shown little ceremony in disposing of any rights that the original inhabitants of those countries which they have discovered and colonized, might have possessed to their native soil; and they have therefore little reason to complain if claims of a similar nature which they may advance are regarded as in some degree variable and uncertain. Indeed, if we look back to the origin of most countries, we shall find that the force which was necessary to conquer, and the ability to defend, were the best titles which the claimants to any territories could assert. In the present day, it is either long possession or purchase which renders such titles of any value. It is difficult to understand how one individual can derive from any natural law a better right than another to the earth which has been given to the whole human race, or to those spontaneous productions which the Almighty has caused to spring up for the benefit of all. So that originally we shall find the conclusion inevitable that it is labour performed at some period or in some manner which gives the real title to property. The justice of giving to individuals a right of property in land arises from the consideration that in no other way can they possess a security that their labour bestowed on the land will be of advantage to themselves. It was predicted as the consequence of the disobedience of the people of Israel to the commands of the Almighty, "Thou shalt build an house, and thou shalt not dwell therein : thou shalt plant a vineyard, and shalt not gather the grapes thereof;" and this state of things would exist in any country where the rights of the owners of the soil were not secured by law, or were liable to invasion by others. The consequence would be, that houses would not be built or vineyards planted. The only property would consist in tents, cattle, and other things that could be removed from place to place without difficulty as amongst the wandering Tartars or Bedouin Arabs.

We may inquire how the circumstances of many parts of the West Indies, and other countries that have only recently been settled by Europeans, are affected by such considerations. It is supposed that any one person acquires a right to ever so large a tract of country, either by purchase, or as a grant from the Government. Unless he can also find means of bringing it into a state of cultivation, he will derive no advantage whatever. He must either labour himself, in which case he will be able to make only a small portion of land available, or he must in some way induce others to labour for his benefit. Now if he can procure slaves, and can by force or by any influence which he can exercise over their minds prevail on them to bestow continuous labour on this land, contenting themselves with what is merely necessary for subsistence, he will be able to procure a large return ; in all probability much more than enough to repay the expenses incurred.

To show that labour employed in the cultivation of land will yield more than is required to supply the necessities of the labourer, we may refer to the state of things which exists in Great Britain. It has been estimated that the total number of families in that country in 1831 were 3,414,175, of those employed in agricultural pursuits 961,134, less than one-third of the whole.

As many of the commodities imported into Great Britain have been rather the conveniences and luxuries than the absolute necessities of life, we may suppose that the agriculturists supplied by far the largest part, not only of that food, without which the population could not subsist, but many other things which slaves seldom obtain, such as a large quantity of animal food, butter, cheese, &c. It is true that they have received in return many manufactered articles, but a people scarcely emerged from barbarism, as the slaves in the West Indies have been, are contented with very little of this kind. We may suppose that had the people employed in agricultural

labour in Great Britain been slaves, and contented to live in
the same way as the negroes in the West Indies have done, at
least one-half of the products of their labour would have gone
as profit to the proprietor. It may be said, however, that
slaves are universally indolent, and that their labour cannot
therefore be as productive as that of free people. If this had
been the case, it is difficult to imagine that less than a million
of people could have supplied the mother country with so
many valuable productions as the West Indies have yielded.
For some time before emancipation the stimulus of coercion
had been gradually losing its efficiency, and no other had
been supplied ; but it is stated that the slaves in Cuba perform
a large amount of labour. It should be remembered that
within the tropics pretty nearly the same labour is performed
at all times of the year, or at least this is the case to a much
greater extent than in countries which are subject to a long
winter. If the labour performed is not very arduous at any
given period, it can be continued with greater regularity than
the seasons admit of in northern climates. Without entering
into minute details, or referring to particular instances, it may
be stated, without fear of contradiction, that property has
seldom yielded larger returns to its owners than West Indian
property during the existence of slavery.

The instance of an individual obtaining possession of a
large tract of land in a newly settled country has been referred to, and it has been shown that if slaves can be procured their labour may be made profitable ; but we shall suppose that it is necessary to obtain the labour of free people.
These free labourers, if they can be induced to remove from
any other country, which is doubtful, as soon as they see about
them an abundance of unoccupied land, will begin to consider whether they cannot obtain a portion for themselves,
and there is little reason to doubt that they can do so, whenever they acquire a moderate amount of capital, on the same
terms as the person who wishes to employ them obtained his.
After they have succeeded in this object, they will generally
find it more profitable and more agreeable to cultivate their own
land than to labour for another, so that the question will not

be, whether free labour is cheaper than slave labour, but whether free labour can be procured at all. We may thus account for the democratic state of society which exists in the United States, unless where slavery gives to the proprietor of land a command over the labour of others.

But if the labour of slaves is so profitable in newly-settled countries, it may be asked why it should not be equally so in the old? If so large a return is obtained from the labour of a comparatively small number of people, why should not a still greater return be obtained from that of a greater number? The reply is, that the return is not derived so much from the labour of the people as from the land, which can only be made available by means of their labour. If slavery existed in Great Britain, it would be necessary for the proprietors of land to provide with the means of subsistence, not only those persons engaged in agriculture, but also those employed in manufactures and commerce, and this they must do from the produce of the soil; so that all their profits would be expended in feeding a superfluity of labourers. To render the latter occupations successful all the skill and ingenuity of the people is required, and for this a state of freedom is necessary. If we were to suppose that moral and religious considerations had nothing to do with the gradual emancipation of the peasantry of the mother country, there is little doubt that the proprietors of land would long ago have been anxious to relieve themselves from the task of supporting them. The difficulty there, is how to provide for the wants of the population, and not how to obtain their labour.

In addition to this, land, like everything else, increases in value from its scarcity; so that its owners have a means of deriving a revenue from its possession without coercing the labour of those who are located upon it. There are so many competitors for the occupation of land, that there is no difficulty in obtaining a fixed rental to the proprietor, and this does not require that constant effort to maintain an authority which renders slavery so annoying a system to all parties concerned. If the occupier of land is unwilling to pay what is demanded of him, another will, in most cases, think it an advantage to

D

do so, if he can obtain the means of subsistence by cultivating the property of another on such terms. Whereas in those countries where land is abundant, there is so much more security in obtaining it as property, that this course, being practicable, will be generally preferred.

These views will be supported by the changes which have taken place in the West Indies since the slaves were emancipated. In Barbadoes the quantity of sugar made in 1832, according to M'Culloch's Dictionary of Commerce, was 266,465 cwt.; in 1841, 257,108 cwt. In Antigua, in 1832, 143,336 cwt.; in 1841, 144,103 cwt. So that in both these islands the crop was very nearly the same after emancipation as before. This may be accounted for by the density of the population, rendering the relations of proprietor and labourer much the same as in the mother country. In Jamaica the sugar made in 1832 was 1,431,681 cwt.; in 1841, 528,585, that is not very far from two thirds less. In Demerara, in 1832, 736,562; in 1841, 415,261. In the two latter places the people have been able to procure land. It will be seen that in Demerara the reduction has not been so great as in Jamaica, but it is probable that much of the labour has been performed by persons introduced from other countries, who could not purchase land until they had acquired by their labour on estates the means of doing so. This will be sufficient to show that where the same quantity of sugar is not made as during slavery, the reduction does not arise from any incapacity in the black man to labour unless under the stimulus of the lash, because in those islands where the population was such as to render the labourer as dependent on the proprietor of the soil as in most countries of Europe, no such falling off in the crop has taken place, at least as the consequence of emancipation. It need not be supposed that in Jamaica or British Guiana there has been any greater amount of indolence than in Barbadoes or Antigua. The labour of the people may only have taken a different direction.

We may ask, then, are the West Indies ruined, or has emancipation proved a failure, because in those places where the people were able to acquire property of their own, they have laboured to a less extent than formerly on the estates of the large proprietors? No doubt these proprietors have sustained a loss, but if this loss had not been expected to occur, would any compensation have been granted? Whether this compensation was sufficient, whether a property in slaves was such that the owners could expect to be completely indemnified for the sacrifice entailed by its annihilation, it is scarcely necessary now to inquire. It may be presumed that this question has been already set at rest, that the owners of estates possessing no longer a claim to the labour of the people have only to consider what is the real value of their land, of the buildings erected, and the improvements made by the investment of their capital. If it is impossible that in the altered state of society these can be made available to the same extent as formerly, it may be a matter for regret. So long as the general interests of the West Indies are consulted, any loss sustained by such persons must chiefly be attributed to their having become identified with a state of things which could scarcely have been perpetuated for any very long period, even if the British Parliament had not interfered to provide for its abolition, and the Colonial Legislatures had not brought the last remnants of the compulsory system to a sudden termination. As certainly as the success of freedom is dependent on the intelligence and good conduct of the people, so the continuance of slavery must be regulated by their willingness to submit to the control of others, instead of asserting the right to think and act for themselves. So soon as they had become impressed with the belief that they had other duties to perform more binding than those which were required of them by their masters, the former system must have become unprofitable, if it had not ceased altogether. Neither Governments nor legislators can say to the progress of the human intellect, " Hitherto shalt thou come, but no farther." If it were proved that there is as close a communication between sugar estates and slavery, as between monasteries and the Roman Catholic religion, it does not follow that it would have been possible to continue the one for the purpose of perpetuating the other. Slavery might have lasted longer, but it might have ceased in a manner less satisfactory.

At the same time it must be considered, that unless there is some security that the possession of property of one kind or another will be advantageous to its owners, there is little prospect that much will be done for the permanent advantage of the West Indies. Such improvements, as it is generally admitted, are required to render the change that has taken place successful, are not likely to be adopted, unless there is reason to believe that those who undertake to introduce them will at least receive a fair return for their expenditure. In many cases they rely on this return for the means of performing their engagements, and if they are disappointed themselves will disappoint others. It may be easy to accuse every one connected with West Indian affairs of mismanagement, and other faults of a like nature, but this does not remedy the evil or show in what it originates. A general state of insecurity, a want of confidence in the success of any undertaking that relates to the future, and a consequent unwillingness to do more than is needed for the supply of the wants of the present moment, can scarcely arise from the abundance of land and the deficiency of labour. If there is a difficulty in obtaining labour we might suppose that all those things on which labour had been already expended, or which tended to its being economised, such as buildings, machinery, &c., would be enhanced in value; and yet this is not found to be the case, at least in some parts of the West Indies. What then is the great evil which involves all the financial concerns, and everything which has a reference to the value and other relations of property in a state of almost inextricable confusion?

Possibly a solution of this problem might be found in the fact that a state of considerable uncertainty still prevails as to the situation in which individuals and communities have been placed by the changes that have been effected. During the continuance of slavery, that property to which the greatest importance was attached, was not the possession of land as in England, but a claim to the labour of others. So soon as this claim could no longer be enforced, the rights of all parties appeared indefinite and incapable of being ascertained with any degree of precision. A reference to some circumstances which occurred on the termination of the apprenticeship will place this matter in a clearer light.

In Jamaica, according to law, the people could only be required to give up their houses and grounds after a notice of three months. To the old people and invalids a longer period was allowed. The question almost immediately arose whether until the expiration of this term any rent could be demanded from them. It appeared desirable that arrangements should be made as speedily as possible, both for rent and for wages, between the free people and their former masters; but for some time it was impossible for both parties to come to any understanding on the subject. As no rent had been paid previously there appeared to be no rule according to which it could be determined what would be a fair demand. In a few instances so much was expected for the land, about four or five acres, occupied by the more industrious people; the pasturage of horses, donkeys, &c., that the wages offered would have been little more than sufficient to afford payment. In other cases no rent was asked. The people were expected to make contracts to remain as servants on the estates, at low wages, the houses, grounds, and other privileges, being regarded as a part of the payment for their labour. As there was little disposition on the part of the labourers to comply with these arrangements, attempts were in some instances made to enforce the payment of rent; but it was maintained by lawyers, who were consulted on the subject, both in Jamaica and in England, that as no engagements had been previously made the demands of the proprietor could not be recognised, and that in case the people were unwilling to pay, the only remedy was to require them to remove as soon as the law permitted. But if 300,000 people insisted on their own terms, any attempt to compel them to give up the houses and land which they had so long occupied might seriously have endangered the peace of the country. On the other hand, as they had the means of subsisting on the produce of the land so long as they remained on the estates, they would have been under very little necessity to work at all if this state of things had been allowed to continue. The settlement of wages was a matter of little less difficulty. The masters had been in the habit of hiring out people, who received from their employers what was considered necessary for their support, and in addition to this from one to two dollars a week, and sometimes even more had been paid to their owners. Such people, on applying for situations, were accustomed to ask for so much wages and so much allowance. The wages were to go to the masters, the allowance to the people for their support. Free people on making engagements, of course, considered themselves entitled to both wages and allowance. The emancipated peasantry expected to be placed on the same footing ; but the proprietors maintained that if this were the case the cultivation of estates could not be continued. Indeed it was scarcely reasonable, as the monopoly of labour possessed by the large proprietors had artificially raised the price. Persons who not possessing slaves, required the services of domestics, and owners of estates who were in need of additional labour in time of crop, or on any other occasion, were obliged to submit to the inconvenience, but it is not likely that for the regular labour required so high a price could have been paid. Many of the persons in whose hands the management of property rested were the agents of proprietors in England, or they were intrusted with the property of minors, so that supposing them to be influenced by no selfish considerations, it was equally incumbent upon them to act honourably to those of whose interests they were the guardians, as well as to respect the rights of the labourers.

Whilst the state of affairs was thus unsettled, the Governor, Sir Lionel Smith, made a tour through the island, for the purpose of giving advice to the people as to their conduct under the altered circumstances. On his visiting a coffee district in the mountains, where some thousands of all classes were collected together, a gentleman, who has since become Speaker of the House of Assembly, stated that he had succeeded in making an arrangement with the people on an estate not far distant, to work for one shilling sterling per day, and to pay back one day's wages in the week as rent for their houses and grounds. These were terms which many of the proprietors maintained that the estates could not afford, at the same time they were

lower than the people generally demanded. The Governor and
the special magistrates present, however, considered them as
fair as any arrangement that appeared practicable under the
circumstances, and strongly advised the people to comply, or
in case other terms were offered to consult the interests of the
country by returning immediately to their work. In a great
number of instances this recommendation was followed by both
parties.

On the sugar estates the wages were usually higher. Objections were made by many persons on behalf of the labourers
to the demand of rent from every member of the family capable
of field labour, but as it was impossible, in the first instance,
correctly to estimate the value of the grounds, taking into consideration the fertility of the soil and other circumstances, it
is probable that as near an approach was thus made to an
equitable system as could have been expected at the time. In
general the quantity of land which the people kept in cultivation was proportioned to their industry, and to the number of
persons whom they had to support. Some time after it was
proposed to a number of labourers, that, instead of giving a
portion of their time as payment of rent, the head of every
family should pay a fixed sum, but the men objected on the
ground that they could not see why their wives should not pay
rent as well as themselves. In cases where both parties insisted
on their own terms, for as long a time as possible, the necessity
for preventing the total loss of the crop of sugar for that year
generally compelled the managers of estates to comply in the
end with the demands of the people. The latter had numbers
on their side, and were in possession of the means of subsistence, so that where they made concessions it was usually as
the result of persuasion rather than force. It was reported that
on one occasion, a gentleman possessing authority in one of
the parishes being requested to procure the appointment of an
additional number of constables, he asked the persons who
made the application whether they wished to bring about a
rebellion? telling them that if they did, the right course to adopt
was to let the people see that they were afraid of them. In
general, the only ground of complaint was that the labourers

did not resume their occupations as readily as their masters desired. No instance of violence of any importance occurred.

The chief difficulty which the managers of property in Jamaica experienced in inducing the labourers to comply with the terms which were proposed to them, arose from the circumstance that the possession of grounds sufficient for their support had been for a long period secured to them by law, and was therefore regarded by them almost in the light of property, of which the master could not with justice dispossess them. Less immediate inconvenience was felt where the practice of allowing them to cultivate land for themselves had not been so general, or carried on to anything like the same extent. Where they were dependent on their masters for subsistence from day to day, this subsistence could be withheld at any moment, so that the necessity of working for wages became apparent. In the smaller islands, such as Barbadoes and others, where the possession of land to any great extent could not be obtained from the density of the population, this dependence on the wages to be obtained by labouring on estates has continued ; but in British Guiana, a disposition to purchase land was soon manifested by the emancipated labourers. From the deficiency of the crop in Jamaica, and in some other places, a rise in the price of sugar almost immediately took place, which operated as a great stimulant to production, and occasioned a competition amongst the proprietors to obtain as much labour as possible, which led to high wages being given. The desire on the part of the people to possess land rendered them more industrious in the first instance than they would otherwise have been, and for some time the state of things appeared prosperous. Even after they had succeeded in procuring land they were for some time dependent on their wages for support, particularly in a country where nothing can be done without drainage, which of course requires time before land newly taken into cultivation can yield a return, as well as for the means of building houses, and making other improvements in their condition ; but these inducements to labour have been gradually diminishing. Africans, Coolies, Madeirans, and others have been brought in to supply the deficiency: so that in many cases the proprietors, instead of trusting to the abour of the native population, have become in a great measure dependent on strangers. This tendency has been increased by the circumstance that where the people could not obtain land in the neighbourhood of the estates on which they had been located, they have often retreated to parts of the country at a distance alike from the estates, the towns, and the places of worship. It appears that the payment of rent has been rare in every part of the West Indies, with the exception of Jamaica. The proprietors have usually evinced a disposition to retain the labourers as servants on the estates, and to allow them many of the old privileges, with a view to obtain a right to their continuous labour. The people have regarded this state of things as something like a perpetuation of slavery, and have been desirous of assuming the position, if not of owners of land, at least of tenants. As it has, however, been generally found impracticable to enforce the claim of the proprietors even to the labour of those who continued on their estates, the permission to remain without the payment of rent has, perhaps, had scarcely any other effect than to lead to a confusion in their ideas as to the rights of property. It might have been just that old people and invalids, who had spent their strength in the service of the estate, should be allowed to retain this privilege, but to young and healthy people it could scarcely have been any real advantage, especially as it could never have been accompanied with anything like security.

In considering the relations of property and labour, it is necessary to refer to another class, comprising nearly the whole of the white and of the educated coloured population of the West Indies, who may be denominated intellectual labourers. Such are the merchants, medical men, ministers of religion, conductors of the press, persons holding government situations, lawyers, attorneys of the proprietors in England, clerks and accountants, persons engaged in the management of estates, and various others. The interests of this class have, probably, been less considered than those of any other. They have frequently been regarded as mere agents, who must, of necessity, carry into effect whatever their superiors might require, and yet there is great reason to think that the future prosperity of these colonies depends on their conduct in a greater degree than on any other circumstances. Should the time ever arrive when the services of such persons would not be regarded as of any utility, when they would not meet with a recompense proportioned to their exertions and ability, it could not be at all beneficial to the more uneducated labourers, who, for want of some persons of superior intelligence to direct their efforts, would probably sink into a state of comparative barbarism, from which it might be centuries before they would emerge. The changes that have taken place in the West Indies have placed these persons, in many instances, in circumstances of embarrassment and difficulty. They are likely to be made responsible for the failure of every unsuccessful undertaking, whilst they are dependent on the Government, the proprietors, and the capitalists in England, for that assistance, without which it appears nearly impossible to render emancipation successful as a measure intended to promote the happiness, as well as the moral and intellectual improvement of the African race. If there is one thing more than another requisite, as a means of promoting the general prosperity, it is that persons of this class should be placed in a situation that would give them some degree of security for a reward, neither dependent on mere accident, nor so fixed as to be unconnected with the success of their own exertions; but exactly proportioned to their intelligence, their energy, and application, as well as the general respectability of character which they evince. Whatever difficulty there may be in rightly estimating the real value of property, the fair return for capital expended, or the proper remuneration for merely mechanical labour, and whatever difficulties and misfortunes may result from a miscalculation on these points, there is little doubt that experience will, sooner or later, lead to their being rightly estimated; but the importance of science, enterprise, ability, and good conduct, can scarcely be determined according to any known standard. It may be desirable to inquire how such qualities are rewarded in those countries that have been most remarkable for their exercise; and whether it is possible that systems which have been found successful elsewhere, are susceptible of an application to the West Indies.

AGRICULTURAL SYSTEM.

There is one essential difference between the agriculture of the West Indies and that which has been pursued in most of the countries of Europe ; that in the former case the productions to which the chief attention has been directed were intended not to supply the wants of the inhabitants, but the wants of the people of the mother country; whilst in the latter it has been considered of the first importance that the inhabitants should provide for their own necessities, and having done so, that they should raise or manufacture such commodities for exportation as would enable them to procure the produce of other countries in return; and yet, strange to say, whilst the population of the West Indies have been so engaged, instead of its being supposed that Great Britain received a benefit from such an application of their labour, it has been taken for granted that by paying for the products of their labour at a higher rate than they might have been procured for elsewhere, she inflicted an injury on her own population, solely for the advantage of the West Indians. If it were possible for the latter to supply their own wants to a greater extent than they have been in the habit of doing, they would be less dependent on an exchange which is no longer to continue on the same footing as heretofore. That they can do so entirely, with any advantage to themselves cannot be expected, but as the principle seems to be admitted that it is the first duty of the people of every country to provide for themselves, there is no apparent reason why the West Indies should be an exception to the general rule. If they raise those things which other countries require, it is not likely they will do so from motives of pure benevolence to those who so far from acknowledging the favour rather consider themselves injured in being compelled to accept it, but simply because in no other way can they make a return for such productions as are necessary to their own comfort and convenience.

But so soon as an attempt is made to reduce this principle to practice a difficulty at once arises. By far the greater proportion of property in many parts of the West Indies, as well as a large amount of capital invested both in trade and in the pursuits of agriculture belongs to persons in England, and are not the rights of such parties to be respected? On this point there can be no question. If property could be purchased, or capital could be repaid, so as to leave those who are now under the control of others, free to take their own course, it might be very desirable, but so long as this is impracticable, nothing can be gained by any conduct that is not in accordance with strict integrity. But the altered state of things has rendered it very difficult to ascertain what are really the rights of parties at a distance who have an interest in West Indian affairs. So long as uncertainty prevails on this point there is scarcely any prospect of a removal of the difficulties which appear to be so general.

From a want of knowledge as to the real value of property many persons have involved themselves in the greatest degree of embarrassment. They have spent the capital which years of industry had enabled them to amass, they have incurred obligations to others, in purchasing what they supposed would yield them a settled income, and they have discovered that so far from their expectations being realised, they were compelled from time to time to advance large sums for the payment of labour and other expenses. They have hoped that some return would be obtained to reimburse them for this outlay, and have found that this *return* has been inadequate, that so far from having anything to receive beyond what they have expended, they have actually incurred a loss, and that, instead of having acquired a real property, they have entailed upon themselves a burden and responsibility with but little prospect even of any ultimate advantage.

It may be said that this is not the general state of things, that wherever it occurs it must have been the result of mismanagement, and that those who are unskilful in the direction of their own affairs have no reason to complain if the consequences are disastrous to themselves. But is it necessary that the possessors of property in the mother country should be remarkably skilled in agricultural pursuits? The tools of a mechanic may be of no value to him who has not ability to use them; but if it were necessary that the noblemen and large proprietors of land in England should be capable of directing the operations of all the farms and manufactories that are carried on upon their land, it is to be feared that many of them would long ago have been involved in far greater difficulties than any of the West Indian proprietors have to complain of. Do they even supply the capital that is necessary to the profitable cultivation of their estates? Are all the cattle and implements of husbandry their property, and intrusted by them to the management of agents, whom they regard as responsible for the failure or success of their concerns? If such a system would not be found successful in England, why should it be supposed to answer better in the West Indies, whilst the proprietor resides at such a distance, that in many instances he has never visited the estates, of which he is not only the owner, but also the farmer, as well as the manufacturer, of the produce derived from them? It is true that the proprietor does not carry on all these occupations personally, but by means of agents; but does the owner of land in England attempt to carry them on at all, or leave them to others, who conduct them, not for the benefit of the proprietor, and as the representatives of his interests, but simply for their own profit and advantage?

It may be asked, why then has such a system as that which prevails in the West Indies been adopted? The answer is that it is quite in conformity with the principles of slavery, which supposes that property does not consist chiefly in land, buildings, and other inanimate objects, but in the labour, skill, and ingenuity of human beings, who are supposed to have no right to consult their own inclinations or their own interests, but simply to labour for another, upon whom they have a claim for the means of subsistence. A story has been related by an old captain of a merchant vessel who had been long in the habit of trading to Jamaica, that many years ago there was a ship which usually went by the name of the Scot's Guineaman; that the captain was in the habit of inducing any boys whom he chanced to meet with in the streets of Perth to come on board his vessel, and then prevailing on them to accompany him to the West Indies. He supplied them with clothing, and everything necessary for the voyage, keeping an account however of the expenses incurred. On their arrival at the destined port, he made an engagement for them with some person who had the management of an estate, from whom he expected payment both of the passage-money, and whatever he might have spent besides on their account. If one of these boys should be unwilling to comply with any requirements that might be made, he was immediately threatened that payment of the debt would be enforced. He was consequently compelled to submit. In this way they were transferred from one to another, in fact sold, until they were able to pay the debt, or by some other fortunate circumstance acquire their freedom. Whatever may be the correctness of this statement, it cannot be doubted that the white people on estates have been kept as completely as possible in a state of subordination; that they have often been dismissed without notice, and generally treated in a manner which rendered them as dependent as possible on those under whose control they were placed. As long as this general system of keeping others in the most complete subjection could be maintained and carried out with anything like consistency, it might at least answer the purposes for which it was intended, but to continue a state of things framed in accordance with slavery, so far as the white people are concerned, after the black are made free, can scarcely lead to any good result.

But desirable as a change in this respect may be, it cannot be denied that there are great difficulties in carrying any such alteration in the management of estates into effect. If the proprietors generally were willing to allow those persons whom they have hitherto employed as their agents to occupy the land and buildings on their engaging to pay a fixed rental for a period sufficiently long to give both parties a security as regards the future, it is doubtful whether there are many persons in some parts of the West Indies in a situation to make such engagements. It is considered that such are the unavoidable expenses of manufacturing either a large or a small quantity of sugar, that an estate which does not yield a very considerable return cannot be made profitable. This was the case even before the late reduction in the price of sugar, and must be so to a far greater extent now. In order to make the requisite quantity, heavy expenses must be incurred. A large number of labourers must be regularly paid. The salaries of the white people employed, the repairs of machinery and other necessary expenses, must be provided for, as well as the rent which the proprietor might claim. On those estates which are at present found to be profitable, the difficulty might not be very great: but in such cases it is probable that the proprietor might think any change unnecessary, or at least would not give up an income which he can receive under present circumstances without an adequate security that he would not be the loser by so doing. Wherever estates do not yield to their owners a return, but rather involve them in expenses which they find it nearly impossible to provide for, there is little doubt that they would be willing, on moderate terms, to allow those persons to occupy them who might have a reasonable prospect, by the application of any energy or resources they might possess, of rendering them profitable. But to restore estates which are already in a declining condition, or the cultivation of which has ceased altogether, it is not merely the regular expenses which must be provided for; a large outlay is required, to bring them into a state to yield any return that would afford a prospect of remunerating the occupier even for the constant expenditure which would be necessary after the capital required in the first instance had been invested. Most of those persons in the West Indies who have succeeded by their industry in accumulating any capital whatever, and these are not a great number, are afraid to embark in any speculation the success of which is so very uncertain as the cultivation of an estate is found to be at present. So many persons have lost whatever they possessed, and involved themselves in the greatest possible difficulties, by a want of caution in such undertakings, that others are discouraged from making any attempts of the kind. So long as those who are engaged in the management of property can receive fixed salaries, or an income which does not involve them in any risk, they will, for the most part, prefer continuing to do so, to seeking a greater degree of independence which must be accompanied with perpetual anxiety, and may possibly be a source of pecuniary loss, which their resources will not enable them to bear without absolute ruin to themselves and those who are dependent upon them. Whenever the state of things becomes so desperate that there is no possibility that the present system can be continued, it is probable that they will prefer removing to another country, and applying their energies in a way that affords some greater security of a result that may be advantageous to themselves. Were their places likely to be occupied by better persons, this might not be so much a matter for regret, but strangers to the West Indies would have the same, and even greater difficulties to encounter, without the advantage of that local experience, the attainment of which is a necessary step towards the success of any undertaking.

In contemplating the possibility of such a removal on the part of the white population of the West Indies, it may not be out of place to consider how the interests of the emancipated peasantry would be affected. There is little doubt that they might provide for their own wants so far as the food absolutely necessary to subsistence is concerned, at least in favourable seasons. But the West Indies are subject to long and severe visitations of drought. Most of the provisions raised by the negroes do not keep for a very long period, and where there is no market to supply such as the residence of the white population affords, they are not likely to be raised in much greater quantity than the people consider necessary for their own consumption. In case of a failure in the crops of plantains, maize, and ground provisions, without the opportunity of working on estates and obtaining the means of supplying themselves from a foreign market, they would be placed in a situation not totally unlike that of the Irish peasantry who have been reduced to so much distress from the failure of the crop of potatoes. But supposing that they could always obtain a sufficiency of food, there are many other things which are necessary to their advancement in civilization, such as clothing, tools, furniture, and other English manufactures.

It is necessary also that the expenses of Government, and the support of ministers of religion and schoolmasters should be provided for. The smallest amount of taxation would become oppressive if it could only be raised from that which is afforded by the provision grounds, even in Jamaica, where they yield a greater variety of productions than in any other part of the West Indies. This would be the case to a far greater extent in British Guiana, where a regular system of drainage is necessary to the comfort and health of the inhabitants, as well as to the productiveness of the soil. Surely those who have considered it a matter of so much importance to procure the abolition of slavery, cannot view without concern any prospect of such a reduction in the exportable productions of the West Indies as would deprive the labouring population of the opportunity of obtaining for themselves those conveniences and advantages of civilized life, the loss of which would render their improvement in intelligence, and even in morals and religion, nearly hopeless, and would place them in a situation similar to that of the ancient Britons when abandoned by the Romans, of the Indians when exposed to destruction by the Spaniards, or of the Tahitians when compelled to yield to the aggression of the French.

These reasonings have, however, been founded on the supposition that an estate, if rented at all, must be rented to a single individual, who would thus incur a liability to heavy expenses with a great uncertainty as to an adequate return. But there may be those who are willing to incur a small risk in the expectation that by a devotion of their energies to that in which they are engaged they may ensure success, when they would shrink from greater liabilities than their resources would enable them to meet. There are also many persons whose abilities are quite equal to the management of small concerns, who must inevitably fail in undertakings of greater magnitude from a want of that comprehensiveness of mind which would enable them to surmount the unexpected difficulties that are

E

sure to be encountered in diverging into a wider sphere than that for which their habits and capacities have fitted them; and of that command over others without which matters ot importance cannot be brought to a successful issue. A comparison between the mode of conducting agricultural operations in the West Indies and that which prevails in the mother country may illustrate this part of the subject. It has been estimated that the number of occupiers of land employing labourers in Great Britain is 187,075, and the number of agricultural labourers 887,167, that is from four to five labourers to one employer. It is calculated that in Jamaica there are 1,693 sugar and coffee estates and pens or farms for raising cattle, and 132,192 agricultural labourers. The number of planters is stated to 3,987. This would give an average of about seventy-eight labourers, and from two to three planters to every estate or pen. In British Guiana the estates are probably much larger, and a greater number of labourers employed on each. It is not to be supposed that all these labourers are at work at one time, but there seems to be no reason why they should not labour with regularity if their necessities required them to do so, or such inducements as appeared to them to be adequate were offered. Now, seventy-eight labourers at one shilling a day, and they could scarcely be expected to work for less, would require that, if they worked for five days in a week, the Saturdays being regarded as market-days, they should be paid nearly £1,000 a year, so that only a large crop of sugar or anything else that might be cultivated would pay this, as well as other necessary expenses. But were the land occupied in smaller quantities, and by persons who would, as in the mother country, engage much fewer labourers, the risk would be small to each employer, and by a more complete superintendence the work might be performed with greater efficiency. Were such persons to be found, it is not by any means improbable that, by the adoption of machinery and a greater employment of intelligence and energy in the direction of the labourers, the land might be rendered so productive as to give an ample return to the proprietor. It is usual to complain that the negroes are less in-

telligent and skilful, as well as less deserving of confidence,
than the labourers of Great Britain; but if this is the case, it
would be natural to conclude that a closer inspection is necessary. So long as slavery continued, although the labour
might not be performed in the best possible manner, wages
were not paid, and the subsistence of the people was not very
costly; but the change that has taken place renders it necessary that the employer should see that the payment is no more
than a fair equivalent for the work. There is no doubt that
persons are to be met with who can superintend a large number of labourers effectually; but, comparing the state of things
in the West Indies with that which exists in the mother country, the inference would be that there is not so much a want of
actual labour as of that diligent superintendence which is
only to be expected where a much larger number of persons
than the white inhabitants of the West Indies are engaged in
attending to those concerns, on the success of which they are
dependent for the means of supporting their families in comfort and respectability. The manufacturing process of sugar
must still be conducted on a large scale, but it will be seen
hereafter that means have been proposed which would render
this perfectly compatible with such a change in the agricultural
system as has here been the subject of consideration.

But as there is a general disposition to persevere in those
plans of operation that have been sanctioned by long usage,
rather than to adopt others that are comparatively untried, it
may be well to inquire whether there is really a necessity for
any important changes of this kind. It frequently happens
that amongst those persons who take an interest in the affairs
of the West Indies, the one class evince a disposition to treat
the complaints that are made by the proprietors as unfounded,
and therefore unworthy of being regarded; and the other is
inclined to solicit that assistance from the Government, which
is rather intended to render the present system successful
than to facilitate any alterations of this kind in the relative
position of the owners of estates, and those whom they employ
as their agents. It is only probable that any such change will
be adopted when its necessity becomes apparent.

It must be remembered that whilst a decline in the productiveness of some West India estates has been going on, a large influx of labourers from the East Indies, Africa, Madeira, and other parts of the West Indies has also taken place. Whatever may be the ultimate results of their introduction, it must be apparent that strangers, having no land of their own, or any means of subsistence beyond what they derive from their labour on estates, have a stronger inducement to work with regularity, at least in the first instance, than the native population. But as very few of the East Indian labourers have brought their families with them, it is generally expected that so soon as the period arrives at which they have been promised a free passage to their own country the greater part of them will return. The Madeirans take the first opportunity of abandoning field labour and establishing themselves in trade. The Africans are as much inclined to purchase land for themselves as the native population, and after having done so, as they are more uncivilised, and therefore less in need of European manufactures, they have less inducement to work for wages. Indeed, it seems to be only for a few years after their introduction that any dependence can be placed on the labour of those persons who are brought from other countries, and it does not appear that anything but a constant supply can benefit the proprietors of estates. Whether it is either possible or justifiable that this should be continued according to the mode at present adopted, is a matter for weighty consideration. In those places where the chief reliance of the planters has been on the native population there is less reason to fear that any decrease in the supply of labour beyond what has been at present experienced will take place. Any improvement in the intellectual capacities of the people is likely both to render them more effective labourers, and also by creating new wants to give additional incentives to industry.

It seems to have been thought by many persons in England that, by restricting the purchase of land, it might be possible to render labour on the estates necessary to the people as a means of supplying their own wants; but to effect anything of this kind it would be necessary not only that the Government should prevent them from acquiring the Crown lands, but that impoverished proprietors, whose necessities require them to obtain money in any possible way, should be prohibited from selling their abandoned estates. To compel the labourers to rest satisfied with a small quantity of land, or to discourage the sale of provisions, would probably have a result just the opposite of what was intended. They would not by any such course be prevented from acquiring the means of subsistence in a manner independent of the large proprietors, which in such places as Jamaica, British Guiana, or Trinidad, it would be almost impossible to deprive them of the opportunity of doing, but merely from obtaining for themselves the conveniences and even the luxuries of civilised life, by exercising their industry in a manner the most in accordance with their own inclinations. It does not follow that if they were prevented from improving their condition in any other way they would labour on the estates. There is greater reason to fear a tendency to idleness and barbarism, than that any kind of industry will be injurious either to the general prosperity of the West Indies or of the proprietors of land.

Notwithstanding all the difficulties which prevail, the time is not yet come for regarding the affairs of the West Indies as hopeless. If there is a general disposition on both sides of the Atlantic to inquire into the causes of the present depression, and laying aside old prejudices and old systems where they are incompatible with the new order of things, to consider fairly what is the best course to adopt, there is little doubt that it may be possible to apply a remedy, but much still remains to be done. It is, however, of the greatest importance to inquire what is practicable. Misdirected efforts may only lead to greater discouragement. So much has been already expended, and so many losses have been incurred, that there is nothing left to waste on doubtful experiments or schemes, that by ending in failure may only lead to still greater disappointment.

Since writing the above, the following intelligent remarks have been observed in a letter signed "Edward Binns," which has appeared in a Jamaica paper. After stating that the possession

of small freeholds had a tendency to encourage apathy and
indolence in the mind of the labourer, the writer proceeds :—

"It is therefore with a view of rousing him from his apathy,
by the force of example of honest industry struggling to
emancipate itself from the thraldom of mere existence, un-
blessed by cultivation, energy, or ambition, that we recommend
encouragement to be given to the small farmer and the man of
small capital. It is a misfortune to have merely two classes,
the very rich and the very poor, in any country—but doubly
so in the West Indies. It was this state of things that ruined
the Roman people, and prostrated the Italian States which had
risen from their ashes, under the chariot wheels of the Spanish
King, and to the present day binds them to the car of the
Austrian Emperor. No nation can be said to be free which
consists of only two classes in the state. There is danger that
the upper will corrupt the lower class, or, what is more likely,
that the lower, being the stronger, will infringe upon the
rights and immunities of the upper, and thus anarchy and
confusion in place of order and regularity become the characteristics of the nation. Hence the necessity of creating a
middle class, which shall interpose a barrier between the others
—the persons composing it being above the temptation of
want on the one hand, and beneath the possibility of corruption
on the other."

INDUSTRIAL IMPROVEMENTS.

In considering what means may be adopted for increasing
the productive capabilities of the West Indies, there is one
fact which it is particularly essential to remember, that the
labourers whose assistance is necessary to the success of all
such plans, are not only free people, but that they are in many
instances rendered comparatively independent by the possession

of land, and that consequently they can neither be controlled by the fear of the lash, as in slave countries, nor by the fear of absolute destitution, as in parts of the world where a scarcity of the means of subsistence places a power in the hands of a portion of the community, such as the landowners of Great Britain, which they may use either for the benefit or the injury of the remainder, according to their own discretion or their sense of justice. It is of no use to inquire whether the state of things which is actually found to exist is favourable or otherwise to the interests of individuals or the welfare of the community ; it is enough to ascertain the fact. An earthquake will not, in conformity with our inclinations, be permitted to overwhelm four-fifths of Jamaica or Trinidad, or nine-tenths of British Guiana, sparing at the same time the inhabitants, in order that the portion of the soil which remains may be rendered more valuable to its possessors. So long as this is not the case, any regulations which either the Government or the proprietors might think fit to impose, are nearly sure to be ineffectual, whilst they serve to create an impression on the mass of the population, that their rulers are desirous of withholding from them those advantages, which a benevolent Providence has designed for their benefit. Neither is it fair to conclude that the desire evinced by the people to obtain as much land as will enable them to provide themselves with the means of subsistence arises from the indolence supposed to be natural to the inhabitants of the tropics. A disposition to acquire property in land is certainly not less conspicuous in England than in the West Indies. It is not only necessary that persons who have no capital should labour to obtain the means of purchasing in the first instance, but after they have succeeded so far, they cannot form new settlements without clearing the mountains or draining the marshes, houses must be built, some means of communication with the more settled parts of the country must be provided, and in all these undertakings it is probable that a greater amount of labour is expended than would be necessary for carrying on the regular occupations which in the time of slavery were performed on estates. The disposition to emigrate westward evinced by the inhabitants, both of the United States and Canada, in all latitudes, is not usually regarded as a proof of their indolence, but of their enterprise and energy. It is a love of independence which influences alike the free citizen of the American Republic and the free negro of the West Indies. There is reason to believe that certain tendencies of human nature are as unalterable as the laws which regulate the movements of the planets, and the changes which take place in the inanimate creation. Wisdom consists not in opposing that which is inevitable, but in so regulating our own conduct as to make that over which we have no control subservient to such objects as we may think it desirable to pursue. Should any one desirous of employing the force of a rapid stream of water, for the purpose of turning a mill, determine to erect his machinery on a neighbouring hill, and then exhaust his energies in stopping up the course of the river, for the purpose of making the water ascend above the level of its source, he might possibly produce a stagnant pool, which being evaporated by the heat of the sun might diffuse pestilence around, but would he obtain the power necessary to the accomplishment of his designs ? It is to be expected that attempts to eradicate those dispositions which the emancipated population of the West Indies have so strongly manifested, and against which no moral principle, or considerations affecting their own interests, can be brought to bear, will be equally fruitless.

But it may be said, that if the peasantry of the West Indies are too independent to find it necessary to labour for others, people must be introduced from other countries who will not be placed in the same situation. But is there any reason why strangers should not be influenced by the same dispositions as the native population ? If they do not return to their own country, will they not acquire an opportunity of gratifying these desires in the course of a few years after their introduction ? It has been seen that in Barbadoes and Antigua the sugar crop has not been materially affected by emancipation, but to render Jamaica as densely peopled as these islands about three millions would be required. The number of inhabitants, according to the last census, was 377,433. British Guiana, of which the population at present is less than one-third that of Jamaica, might support at the same rate about thirty millions. Now, if these could be introduced at so small an expense as that of £10 a head, where are the three hundred millions to come from to pay for their importation ? And if they were to be conveyed backwards and forwards at the end of every five years, as it is proposed to do with the East Indians, would Great Britain itself be able to support the expenditure ? Surely the idea of so increasing the population of the larger West Indian settlements, as to produce that dependence of the labouring classes on the proprietors of the soil which exists in the mother country and in the smaller islands, must be abandoned as impracticable, or at least not likely to meet with accomplishment for centuries !

But supposing that labourers to anything like this extent could be obtained. It would be necessary that improvements in civilization and in habits of industry should keep pace with an increase in the population, or the people would only raise what was necessary for their own subsistence, and in this case the proprietors of the soil would reap no advantage. The most oppressive systems of government could not take from any people that which they do not possess. The wealth of the landowners in England is a consequence of the general wealth of the country, and this again arises from the intelligence, enterprise, and energy of the inhabitants. It must, therefore, be evident that to foster these qualities is a matter of much greater importance than to introduce a destitute population, who must be fed, attended to in sickness, and otherwise provided for, if any attention is to be paid to the dictates of humanity, and who possibly may not labour, even to the extent that is necessary, for their own support, to say nothing of their repaying the cost of their introduction. Unless they do this, a loss to the community must result, whatever advantage may be gained by individuals.

The great dependence of the planters at present appears to be the demand on the part of the people for English manufactures, and money to pay for medical attendance, education, and other things which they require. It is not likely that wants of this kind will diminish. It is more probable that they will increase with the general advancement of society. For a long time to come it must be more advantageous that the West Indies should receive such supplies from other countries as well as wheat, flour, and some other things which the white inhabitants regard as necessary in exchange for their agricultural produce, than that they should begin to manufacture for themselves to a greater extent than circumstances afford any facility for their doing. Beyond what is required for the attainment of these objects it is nearly impossible to calculate on the labour of the people. But the inconvenience chiefly complained of is, that as they obtain food principally from their grounds, and as they do not feel the necessity of working for their whole time to supply their other wants, the labour which they give to the estates is irregular and uncertain, and also that their employers do not possess a sufficient control over them to secure an efficient performance of those tasks for which they are actually paid. From these circumstances many estates have been found so unprofitable that their cultivation has been entirely abandoned. For such a state of things it is extremely desirable to endeavour to provide a remedy.

Of all the plans for promoting industry, and increasing the productiveness of the soil, probably the one most in conformity with a state of freedom, and with the love of independence so generally evinced, is that which has attracted general attention in Jamaica, the establishment of public mills. If this can be accomplished it will be unnecessary for every individual proprietor to keep in order large and expensive machinery, and to carry on agricultural operations on a scale so extensive as to render the working of this machinery advantageous. It will be practicable for all persons of intelligence, whatever may be their colour, who are capable of directing labourers successfully to adopt those modes of cultivation which are best suited to their resources and abilities. The discipline of a sugar estate, which it seems nearly impossible to maintain, without a greater control over large numbers people than appears consistent with the altered relations of labourers and employers, will become unnecessary. The motives for exertion will undergo a decided change. If those persons who now manage property as the agents of others can either become the owners or the occupiers of land by paying fixed rental for a term of years, without being compelled to engage in undertakings beyond their resources, and to incur expenditure which they are unable to meet, but by placing themselves in a situation of great pecuniary embarrassment, the consciousness that their success will be proportioned to their own intelligence, activity, and good management, will give them the strongest inducements to exercise whatever abilities they possess to the utmost, which they can scarcely be expected to do so long as they feel that the loss incurred by failure will fall not on themselves, but on the proprietor, and that anything gained as the result of their exertions will not increase their incomes, but that of the possessor of the land. Their situation being one of greater security, and less dependent on the will of others, they will be able to make arrangements for bringing up respectable families, such as have a tendency to introduce an improved tone of morals into West Indian society. The need which such persons will feel of a better class of educational establishments may induce individuals of superior attainments to devote themselves to the work of supplying necessities of this kind, so as to render it no longer imperative on those parents who wish to provide their children with instruction suited to their station in the community, to send them to England, for so long a period, that, on their return, they often regard their nearest relatives as strangers, whilst the want of parental influence has rendered school education nearly ineffectual in developing those affections and principles which form the best security for respectability of character through life. The healthiest localities might be selected for carrying on such establishments, and there is little doubt that young persons so trained would be better able to encounter an exposure to heat, as well as the numerous difficulties which are peculiar to a tropical climate, than those who are either natives of a colder country, or who by long residence in the earlier part of their lives, have become habituated to circumstances totally unlike those, the influence of which they are destined for the future to undergo. As regards religion, a position of comparative independence, without that degree of affluence which relieves its possessor from the necessity for much exertion either mental or physical, produces a feeling of responsibility which deepens the sense of moral obligation, both towards the Creator and to our fellow-creatures, on which all religion is founded.

Those who are placed under the absolute control of others, are inclined to suppose that whatever may be the effects of their conduct, the fault is not theirs, but that those under whose direction they have acted are to blame. Not being able to carry out their own convictions, reflection appears to be useless, and however conscious they may be that the course they adopt is not in conformity with right principles, the idea that a change of conduct is impracticable leads them rather to avoid such conclusions, by diverting the attention to objects of mere pleasure and amusement than cordially to set about the work of reformation. It may be easy to censure the conduct of others, but if systems are adopted unfavourable to moral improvement, those who maintain these systems, because they regard them as advantageous to themselves, are chiefly responsible.

It is not only in regard to the white and the educated coloured inhabitants of the West Indies, that such a change from the relation of proprietor and agent to that of servant and landlord, as a separation of the manufacturing process of sugar from that which is purely agricultural, would be likely to produce, might be expected to operate beneficially. The more intelligent black people, and those who already possess to a certain extent the advantages of education, might occupy land on the same terms. They would imitate not only the modes of cultivation adopted by their better instructed neighbours, but their household arrangements, furniture, and manner of living, and would in their turn become the objects of imitation to those below them in the scale of society. Their increased expenditure would be a motive to greater exertions both of the mental faculties and the physical energies. Whilst they continue mere labourers, the independence of their circumstances will inevitably render them inefficient and intractable; but whenever the superior class of negroes assume the position of small farmers, a desire to rise in the social scale, to exercise that political influence which their position will give them wherever a system of representative government is adopted, and to meet as much as possible on terms of equality with their neighbours, who are distinguished from them by little else than a lighter complexion, will bring their capacities into exercise, and in all probability render them useful members of society.

It may be necessary here to reply to objections to such a change in the social position of the labouring population of the West Indies, that have sometimes been made by persons extremely desirous of promoting their religious improvement. It has been said that such an occupation of the mind in worldly concerns as would thus be produced would be an obstacle to that spirituality which the Scriptures enjoin ; that such passages as "Take no thought, saying, What shall we eat ? or, what shall we drink ? or, wherewithal shall we be clothed ?" should be attended to, and put in practice. The reason given, however, for not taking thought about things of this kind, was not that they were unnecessary or undesirable, but that "your heavenly Father knoweth that *ye have need* of these things." It is stated expressly, "Seek ye first the kingdom of God, and his righteousness, and *all these things shall be added unto you.*"

It does not appear that the intention was to point out that objects of this kind were undeserving of effort, but to show in what manner they might be attained most effectually, that is by seeking first the kingdom of God and his righteousness. If it were possible to arrive at that devotedness to the concerns of eternity, which would render everything earthly of little importance in comparison, it might be desirable ; but in those countries where Christianity is supposed to possess the greatest influence over the character do we find that any such result is produced ? Indolence, and a state of mental inactivity, can scarcely be regarded as favourable to religious improvement. The subjects which are brought before the attention in Scripture cannot be understood without a habit of reflection and diligent inquiry. Those who are not accustomed to exercise their thoughts about any object whatever, find the effort of mind thus required both wearisome and painful. It is usually found in Great Britain, that the middle class of society, whose wants are such as to render a close attention to their worldly affairs absolutely necessary, are the most constant in their religious observances, and the most active in promoting objects of charity and benevolence. It is impossible to contrast the desire which the negroes evince for commodious and even elegant places of worship, the readiness with which they have given their money for such objects, and the neatness of their dress on Sundays, with the carelessness which they evince especially in British Guiana, in reference to their own houses and their dress on ordinary occasions, without arriving at the conclusion that there is a connexion between religion and the improvements of civilised life, and that just when they are engaged about the one they show the greatest solicitude in reference to the other. Even a love of excessive finery can scarcely have so injurious an effect on the character as an extreme negligence in regard to dress and household arrangements. The former is an evil which is very likely to correct itself. Wherever gay and expensive ornaments, a showy equipage, and other things of a like nature are regarded as the exclusive privilege of the higher classes, they are sought for as a mark of distinction. When they become generally attainable they are avoided as a proof of false taste, and neatness, propriety, and extreme cleanliness, become the distinguishing characteristics of superior rank. The fondness for show and ornament, on the part of the black people, is already producing this effect in the West Indies. The more educated classes are usually distinguished by the plainness of their dress, especially in places of worship. In this respect they are sure to be imitated by those who regard them as examples, and in this way a desire for excessive ornament is likely soon to be banished altogether. Consistency and propriety of dress is one of those marks of improvement which it is perhaps most desirable to introduce. It is intimately connected with a right discharge of the duties which the various members of families owe to each other. So long as the men cook and wash their own clothes, and the women labour in the field for their own support and that of their children, anything like order and cleanliness must be impracticable; but whenever they become less selfish, and more inclined to assist one another, a division of labour takes place. Individuals by confining themselves to their own proper duties perform them with greater regularity and precision, and the effect on their general circumstances and relations one to another is at once apparent.

The improvement of roads is a subject closely connected with that of public mills and the changes which their erection may be expected to produce on the general state of society. Indeed, it is indispensable if the canes are to be brought from a considerable distance to any one spot, that an improved mode of conveyance should be adopted. Those who are practically acquainted with the circumstances of particular localities must be the most capable of judging in what manner this object can best be effected. One great obstacle to undertakings of this kind is the expense with which they must in the first instance be attended, and the doubts which are entertained as to their becoming ultimately profitable. It is also a question, by what parties this expense should be incurred, and in what hands the management should be placed. Individuals or companies can scarcely be expected to run any great risk for the general advantage. It is probable that the establishment of such public mills, and the construction of the roads necessary to render them available, would more immediately benefit the proprietors of the land in their neighbourhood than any other parties, by creating a demand for any soil fitted for the growth of canes, which might be brought to the factory, and either sold, or the sugar returned to the agriculturist on payment of the expenses of the manufacture. The profits of such establishments to those by whom they are brought into effect, might not be immediate, as time is required for the introduction of new systems; but if they were regarded as secure, and the objects which it is designed to accomplish of general utility, there is little doubt that all difficulties might, in one way or another, be overcome, whether any applications that may be made for assistance from the government should prove successful or otherwise.

As an impression seems to have been entertained, by some parties in England, that it would be more practicable to send home the juice of the cane, and to carry on the process of manufacturing sugar in England, it may be well to notice, that as machinery on estates would still be required for extracting the juice and bringing it to such a state of condensation as would be necessary for its exportation, such a plan would not effect that entire change in the general system of agriculture that would result from the growing of canes becoming entirely separated from the manufacture of sugar. If the latter process were to be carried on partly in the West Indies and partly in England, it is possible that loss instead of gain might result, and without any corresponding advantage.

The construction of the railroad between Kingston and Spanish Town in Jamaica, and the fact that another railroad is in progress in British Guiana with every prospect of success, may serve to show that undertakings of this kind are not so impracticable in the West Indies as some persons might be disposed to imagine. The rapidity with which places of worship are frequently erected affords reason for the conclusion that the negroes are more willing to give their labour for the execution of designs which they believe to be for the general advantage, than where they are merely influenced by a desire to supply their own necessities. If they imagine "that the country will be spoilt," or that "the slave people will get an advantage of them," they will exert themselves to prevent anything so disastrous with much greater energy than merely to serve the interests of an individual proprietor whom they cannot suppose to be in want of so much money as they imagine that the sugar raised on an estate will produce. Their ideas on subjects of this kind are extremely singular, as, for instance, when the attempt was first made to induce them to take copper money, or what they termed the brass farthings, in payment of their wages, they evinced the greatest unwillingness to do so. A man who had been asked what was the reason for this objection, replied, " That the brass farthings would make the people poor; that the people in England were so poor because they took them, and that if they took the brass farthings, by-and-bye all the country would come poor like England." It would not be very difficult to convince them that the erection of public mills in which their canes could be made into sugar as well as those of the large proprietor, and the construction of roads for affording a better communication for this purpose, would be likely to make the country rich rather than poor, and they might thus be induced to labour with greater assiduity for the furtherance of such an object.

An improved system of drainage has been regarded as of the utmost importance in British Guiana. In addition to the large canals and trenches for carrying off the superfluous water, the fields in that country are intersected with small open drains within a few feet of one another. So long as this is the case it is found that the plough cannot well be used; indeed it has been tried in several instances, but apparently without much success. To obviate this difficulty, it has been recommended that covered drains should be adopted, which being underneath the soil would render it practicable that cattle and machinery should perform that labour for which a large number of people have hitherto been regarded as necessary. Until now it has appeared doubtful whether the advantage would be a sufficient compensation for the great expense which must be incurred. At the present time it is particularly desirable that any plan which affords a prospect of the substitution of machinery for manual labour should be attempted without delay.

The obstacles to cultivation in a country liable to inundations, not only of fresh water from the interior, but also of the sea from the rising of the tides, are less injurious to the proprietor, from the circumstances that the people in their provision grounds have the same difficulties to encounter, with less facilities for adopting that regular system by which they may be overcome. The canals which are rendered necessary by the lowness of the land also serve for the conveyance of canes to the manufactory.

The expenditure which must be incurred in taking new land into cultivation, probably tends to give to those estates which are once brought into a thriving condition a greater value than they would otherwise possess, but those persons who attempt to

F

carry on any kind of cultivation with insufficient capital suffer severely from the certainty that a large outlay is indispensable before any return can be expected. Could means be adopted for relieving such parties from the pressure of the difficulties with which they are surrounded, it would be of the greatest advantage.

In concluding this part of the subject, it is only justice to allude to the encouragement given by Lord Elgin to agricultural societies in Jamaica, and indeed to the expression of opinion in regard to everything likely to promote the general welfare of the West Indies. The influence exerted in that island has extended itself to other places. In Barbadoes and Antigua simultaneous operations have been carried on.

An agricultural chemist, of superior attainments and remarkable for diligent application, Dr. Shier, has been induced to enter on a residence of some years in British Guiana for the purpose of endeavouring to ascertain what improvements may be introduced with any prospect of success, and of giving the inhabitants the benefit of his researches.

It is only by a constant attention of those who possess information and experience to subjects of this character, and a general diffusion of knowledge, that a discovery of the right means for placing countries in which there are so many difficulties to be overcome in a position to sustain the competition to which they are exposed can possibly be made. A large amount of human happiness may result from success, whilst not only the freedom of the African race, but the prospects of improvement of many other races in similar circumstances, would be materially retarded were the friends of humanity in every part of the world to be discouraged by failure in this instance, after the hopes that have been entertained, and the efforts that have been made for the accomplishment of an object so noble and so well worthy the attention of every friend to the welfare of the whole human species. An ultimate failure we cannot anticipate, but success may be materially retarded either by misdirected efforts or by apathy and indifference to the work that still requires to be performed.

It is difficult to understand why the works that are at

present in operation should not be converted into public mills without any great expense being incurred, and it is now pretty certain that they would be sources of profit to those who established them.

NOTE TO PAGE 27.

That this view is entertained in Jamaica is apparent from the establishment of a Proprietary School under the patronage of his Excellency the Governor. The Vice-Presidents are the Lieutenant-Governor, the President of the Council, the Lord Bishop, the Chief Justice, and the Speaker of the House of Assembly. The following announcement will show the views entertained by the promoters of this undertaking:—

"At the present moment, when public attention is so generally directed to education, it has become a subject of serious regret that there are no schools in the island capable of receiving the children of the upper and middle classes of society. This want has hitherto been supplied by sending their children at an early age to England, but besides the moral evils of separating children from their parents entirely, the effects of which many have had cause to lament, it is evident that in the altered circumstances of the island very few will be able to continue so expensive a system. It is, therefore, most desirable to attempt the introduction of some better plan for the future, and none seems more likely to succeed than the formation of a Proprietary School, similar in its object to those successfully established in England, in which the plan of education will combine, together with the study of the classics, mathematics, and modern language, sound theological teaching according to the doctrines of the Church of England, and watchful care over the health and morals of the pupils."

The duties of life being performed from a desire to do that which is right in itself and acceptable to the Almighty, the result would be more beneficial, even so far as the worldly interests of the individual were concerned, than where an anxiety to procure food and raiment was the chief motive for action.

CONCLUDING CHAPTER.

THERE are still three chapters of Mrs. Campbell's work unpublished. They relate to foreign trade and trade with the
mother country, internal trade, and local government

The late Lords Grey and Holland, aided most ably by
Lords Derby, Brougham, Monteagle, Glenelg, Carlisle, and John
Russell, and inspired with courage by the Parliament and the
country, aimed to secure, so far as the government of that day
could do it, freedom to all the slaves in the British Colonies,
and if the exertions of some of their successors have not kept
pace with the public expectations, or the positive requirements
of the colonists, it has, no doubt, been owing rather to the
want of sound and accurate information than to indifference or
want of ability.

The government of the Earl of Aberdeen, and the Duke of
Newcastle, aided by Lord John Russell, have now an opportunity, which they cannot allow to escape without improvement. Both Parliament and people will heartily approve and
second their efforts to enable the colonists to overcome their
difficulties, and to establish freedom and prosperity on an im-
movable basis.

The colonies require that the interference of the government
of the mother country, and the exercise of the authority of
their Sovereign, should depend, not on the caprice of whoever
may happen to be Colonial Minister, but on some fixed and
equitable principle. They have a right to be treated as British
subjects; to be fairly represented in the Imperial, or their own
Parliaments; to be governed by law; to have the same protection; the same facilities for approaching their Sovereign;
and the same advantages in regard to diminished taxation of
their produce, and pecuniary assistance in their attempts to
drain their estates, as have been cheerfully conceded to landowners in Great Britain.

On what principle, they may fairly ask, is it that a tax should be imposed on the produce of their cultivated land, far, very far, exceeding that imposed on the produce of land in England ? Or, that, whilst every landowner in this country who desires to improve his estate by thorough drainage; and can give adequate security, can obtain assistance from the Government to enable him so to do at a moderate interest, repaying the principal by instalments, the West Indian landowner cannot, however good his security may be, obtain the same assistance, if he requires to increase his sugar cultivation, or what would be of equal importance, plant cotton for the supply of our manufacturers on his coast-lands ? As to loans for emigration purposes on the security of the taxes, that is not what is required.

Could he obtain a diminution of the rate of duty on his sugar, and the ability to drain his lands by means of the admirable and economical plough for thorough draining land, the invention of Mr. Fowler, he would be able to double or treble his crop, whilst a diminution of the duty on his sugar would greatly increase its consumption, and enable him very speedily to drive the slave-owners out of the market. It is calculated, too, that the coast-lands of Jamaica, Demerara, and Berbice, if put into cotton cultivation, would yield at least one hundred and fifty million pounds of cotton annually. Is it safe for our cotton manufacturers to depend entirely on slave-owners for their supply of a staple on which, not only the value of their own mills and machinery depend, but also the profitable employment of the tens of thousands of men, women, and children who earn a competency in those mills ? How long do they think American slavery is to last ? Where could they now find, where have they in past times found, better customers than the West Indians ? What of profitable manufactures does a slave consume in proportion to a free man or woman ? If we made our own colonies prosperous, as they might easily and speedily be made, the Americans, the Spaniards, and the Brazilians would soon find it to be their interest to free their slaves, whose needs as freemen would vastly exceed their demands when in bondage.

Great improvements have been already made, and others are now making, in the manufacture of sugar ; but I have seen or heard of none equally simple, economical, and well adapted to the colonies, with those of Mr. Bessemer. If Mr. Fowler's draining-plough, Mr. Bessemer's evaporating and cleansing machinery, and the draining engines which have been employed with so much success to remove the surplus water from the draining trenches of British Guiana in the rainy season, could be brought into general use on the estates of British Guiana. Trinidad, Jamaica, and Dominica, they would tend more than anything else, that I have thought or heard of, to restore prosperity to all these colonies. When the coast-lands are cleared and drained, these countries will become healthy, and when that is the case, voluntary emigrants and persons of capital will take up their residence there, for this simple reason, that the virgin land and deep alluvial soils of these countries are far better adapted to the cultivation of the sugar-cane, and the finest descriptions of cotton, and many other things, than the Southern States of America, whence we now derive our largest supply of cotton. From a statement made on the authority of the President of the Council of Montserrat, in the annual returns lately laid before Parliament, it appears, that the profit, even in that island, on the cultivation of an inferior kind of cotton, estimated to yield only seven pence a pound, was nearly 100 per cent. on the whole expenditure.

It is well known that cotton has been cultivated in Berbice within the last forty years, so as to yield a net profit of £18 sterling per acre, and there is reason to believe that it would now, on properly drained land, yield at least thirty per cent. per annum on the capital employed. And as it regards sugar, it is asserted by Governor Barkely, on what he considers very high authority, viz. that of Dr. Shier, the agricultural chemist, that were the lands of Guiana, thorough-drained, and properly tilled and manured, they would produce three times as much sugar as in their present state, and that at very little extra cost.

Dr. Shier reports that " by reason of the lowness of the land, and the plan of drainage in use, viz. that known as the open-drain and round-bed method, the system of cultivation (in

British Guiana) remains exactly as in the times of slavery, every part of the operations of cultivation being performed by manual labour. The plough and other implements have been tried, but cannot succeed in securing a cheap and effective tillage, till a system of close or covered drainage is resorted to, and the open drains are abolished. Almost the only implements of tillage in use are the shovel, the hoe, and the cutlas. The tillage in general is of the rudest kind, and were it not for the unparalleled fertility of the soil, nothing like the results actually obtained could be conceived possible. There is no such thing known as clearing or fallowing a field, so as to get it into good tilth, and free of weeds, or the seeds of weeds, before planting. There is no alternation of crops, no manuring, but a field once planted, although at the time full of weeds, continues to be cultivated for a great number of years, new plants being put into the blanks that appear at the time of its being examined immediately after the canes are cut. The tillage, improperly so called, is very slight, and consists of a little digging in the neighbourhood of the cane-rows, called shovel-ploughing, and this is not always given every year." "Were this system of drainage improved, so as to admit of cattle and implemental labour, and were a mixed system, in which the rearing and feeding of cattle formed a part, and a judicious system of manuring adopted, there is good reason to believe that three times our present returns would be secured, and that at little greater cost than at present."

Can any reasonable man then doubt, that if the draining plough, with steam power, were generally adopted, cattle, consequently, used where men and women are now employed, and the new system of sugar manufacture and public mills, suggested in the preceding pages, generally introduced, that the cultivation of estates by means of free labour, aided by science, would speedily drive the slave-owners out of the market, and induce them to " let the oppressed go free," for want of means to maintain costly, as well as iniquitous, management ? Let the Government, the Parliament, and the haters of slavery, in the senate, on the platform, and through the press, heartily cooperate with the wise and benevolent in the Colonies, to introduce such improvements as have been pointed out, with a view, not alone to the restoration of prosperity to the West Indian colonists, but also to put an end to slavery by the most legitimate and practicable means ; and then they may fairly expect to see, even in their times, the fulfilment of one great end of the appearance of the Redeemer in our world, which was " to break every yoke," and proclaim " deliverance to the captives, the acceptable year of the Lord." If by action, by endurance, or by these pages, we shall have contributed in the slightest degree to encourage and stimulate our countrymen and women to united exertions in this good cause, our labours will not have been, on the whole, unsatisfactory to ourselves.

S. B.

Brixton, Surrey, April 13, 1853.

THE

IMPORTANCE, NECESSITY, AND PRACTICABILITY

OF

THOROUGH DRAINAGE

IN

THE BRITISH WEST INDIA COLONIES

IN ORDER TO RESTORE

PROSPERITY TO THOSE COUNTRIES;

AS WELL AS TO

RENDER COMPULSORY LABOUR UNNECESSARY TO THE

PRODUCTION OF AN ADEQUATE SUPPLY

OF

SUGAR AND COTTON.

A LETTER

TO

THE RIGHT HON. THE EARL OF ABERDEEN,

BY A LATE

STIPENDIARY MAGISTRATE IN JAMAICA.

LONDON :
THOMAS BOSWORTH, 215, REGENT STREET.
1853.

LONDON:
G. J. PALMER, SAVOY STREET, STRAND.

THE BRITISH WEST INDIA COLONIES.

My Lord,

No one who is acquainted with your Lordship's character will question your determination to promote the honour of the Crown and the welfare of the people of this great empire, by every means in your power; and if any one of her Majesty's subjects, or, indeed, of your fellow men, thinks he can point out any means by which the one or the other may be advanced or secured, I am sure he need offer no apology to your Lordship for attempting it. In former years a large quantity of the finest description of cotton was imported into this country from British Guiana, whereas we now depend almost entirely on the slave states of America for the supply of our cotton manufactures. The quantity of sugar now imported into this country from the British West India Colonies, although larger than in some former years, is not by any means sufficient to supply the demand; and both for cotton and sugar, therefore, we are compelled to resort to slave-owners. This appears to me to be owing to a want of due consideration on the part, not only of our rulers, but of the people; and especially that portion of them who most cordially hate slavery, but do not at the same time exert themselves in the most effectual way to put it down. That way would be to render our colonies prosperous. But how, it may be asked, can this be done? I answer, " By doing to others, as we would have others do to us." The legislators of this country are necessarily landowners. To guard against the temporary evils which were apprehended from free trade, it was thought advisable, as well as just, to enable the proprietors of the soil in Great Britain to improve the estates, assist the farmers, and increase the quantity of produce, by draining their farms, and for this purpose to obtain loans on the security of their properties. Exactly the same thing is required, by the proprietors of land in the West Indies; and since they are our fellow-subjects, since they can produce articles as necessary to the employment and comfort of our own people as the British agriculturists, and since they are engaged in a struggle more trying and arduous than our landowners and farmers, there seems no good reason why the same kind of aid should not be afforded to them.

When twenty millions of money were granted to the owners of slaves, as compensation, it was not given to the legislatures or governments of the respective colonies to be disposed of as they thought fit, but directly to the owners of the slaves, through Commissioners appointed by the Crown. Why should not the same method be adopted in re-

4

gard to thorough drainage? Why should not a man, who has an estate, which may have cost him ten thousand pounds, and would give him a most handsome return for his capital, skill, and labour if it were thorough-drained, have the same opportunity that the English, Scotch, or Irish landowners have of obtaining assistance to enable him to effect this object, if he is in a position to offer to Commissioners, on whose discretion and integrity reliance can be placed, good and sufficient security for the repayment of the same? I can conceive no good reason. If he wishes to import labourers from Calcutta, or China, or Africa, many of whom die on the passage, and many more in the country, the Government is ready to assist him with loan or guarantee. Why not do the same to enable him to put his land in a condition in which he may use cattle and implements instead of men? Why, if he can thus double or treble his crops, and give a greatly increased value to his estate, not enable him to do so?

In an Appendix to the first Report of the Ceylon and British Guiana Committee to the House of Commons, there is a petition (p. 357, No. 18) from the Court of Policy and the Financial Representatives of British Guiana, to the Imperial Parliament. From that petition the following is an extract:—

" That your petitioners beg most earnestly to call the attention of your Honourable House to the fact, that the system of drainage in universal use in the colony, is only adapted to a state of society such as existed prior to emancipation, when manual labour for every field operation was abundant, effective, and cheap.

" That this system of draining, known as the open-drain and round-bed system, compels the sugar growers of the colony to continue a method of cultivating their fields by manual labour, which is the dearest, and which moreover is inefficient as compared with methods employed by other colonies. That this system is altogether incompatible with the employment of cattle labour, the use of the most approved agricultural implements, and with the introduction of the numerous improved methods of agriculture so well known elsewhere, and which, but for this obstruction, the proprietors of estates in the colony would at once gladly adopt.

" That the present system of drainage is, on a large majority of estates in the colony, incompatible with the production of sugar of average quality and colour, by reason chiefly of the large quantity of saline matter which exists in the soils, and from which they cannot be freed by the ordinary method of draining. That the presence of this saline matter, moreover, entails on proprietors of estates an amount of loss, by drainage of sugar and molasses on shipboard, during the homeward voyage of their produce, which greatly reduces their profits, and renders the acknowledged fertility of the soil and fecundity of the climate to a great extent unavailing.

" That your petitioners can show, that were the sugar growers of this colony enabled to adopt a more perfect system of drainage, admitting of the ' thorough drainage' of the land by close or covered drains, and laying flat the surface of the cane-fields, most of the difficulties under which they at present labour would be obviated."

The petitioners state, that " six adult labourers in Scotland, with the aid of four horses, two ploughs, &c., are known to labour 100 acres on the four-course rotation; whereas, to cultivate 100 acres land, and manufacture the produce, in British Guiana, 50 negroes, working well and continuously, are required." "Allowing that cane cultivation and the manufacture of sugar might require double the number of hands needed for 100 acres of land in Scotland," the petitioners state, " that four horses, two ploughs, and corresponding implements would effect a saving of 38 out of 50 labourers, a saving," as they state, "which it is obvious that no measure of immigration can possibly supply to the colony at the same cheap rate, even were it otherwise equally valuable."

The petitioners, amongst other advantages, state, that "improved drainage and cultivation of the soil would be found to prevent disease, to moderate the virulence of epidemics, and to improve the general health of the community."

Amongst other names of the highest respectability this Petition bears those of William Arrindell, Chief Justice, Peter Rose, John Croal, James Stuart, and Thomas Porter, Jun.

Another Petition containing similar allegations, bears the names of nearly every considerable proprietor, attorney, planter, and merchant in the colony.

In a despatch from Governor Barkely, dated April, 1852, there appears as follows :—

" 36,271 acres of canes were cut last year to make 46,335 hogsheads of sugar, or about a ton per acre. This is, nevertheless, far below what might be obtained with better drainage, and a higher system of cultivation, judging from the uniform fertility of the soil, and the yielding of the canes under favourable circumstances. In fact, a most competent judge, Dr. Shier, late Agricultural Chemist of this colony, states it as his opinion, that three times the present return might be secured and at little greater cost than at present."

Dr. Shier himself thus describes the system of agriculture at present pursued in British Guiana :—

" By reason of the lowness of the land, and the plan of drainage in use, viz., that known as the open-drain and round-bed method, the system of cultivation (in British Guiana) remains exactly as in the times of slavery, every part of the operations of cultivation being performed by manual labour. The plough and other implements have been tried, but cannot succeed in securing a cheap and effective tillage, till a system of close or covered drainage is resorted to, and the open drains are abolished. Almost the only implements of tillage in use are the shovel, the hoe, and the cutlas. The tillage in general is of the rudest kind, and were it not for the unparalleled fertility of the soil, nothing like the results actually obtained could be conceived possible. There is no such thing known as clearing or fallowing a field, so as to get it into good tilth, and free of weeds, or the seeds of weeds, before planting. There is no alternation of crops, no manuring, but a field once planted, although at the time full of weeds, continues to be cultivated for a great number of years, new plants being put into the blanks that appear at the time of its being examined immediately after the canes are cut. The tillage, improperly so called, is very slight, and consists of a little digging in the neighbourhood of the cane-rows, called shovel ploughing, and this is not always given every year." " Were this system of drainage improved, so as to admit of cattle and implemental labour, and were a mixed system, in which the rearing and feeding of cattle formed a part, and a judicious system of manuring adopted, there is good reason to believe that three times our present returns would be secured, and that at little greater cost than at present." *

In a lecture delivered to the Demerara Agricultural Society, a copy of which was forwarded by the Governor to the Colonial Office, Mr. Field stated, that " sometimes the soil is sour from bad drainage, the canes will not then ripen, with all the assistance of sunshine. Sometimes, again, the soil is rank from being new and having too large a proportion of vegetable matter ; the cane then has such an abundance of acid and nitrogenous matter that the sugar is black and of very diminished value. The manure required to counteract these causes are the cane-ash, burned earth, coarse sand, lime, and gypsum. I must premise, however, that manure, with surface-drainage, will lose much in quantity and effect. The rain will carry it off the top of the land into the small drains, and from the thinness of the soil there it will not be retained long in its substance. With thorough drainage, good tilling, and an addition of these manures, I have no doubt our soil would produce regularly, even with our present amount of manual labour, three to five hogsheads of sugar per acre." " No. 49, on the Courantyne Coast, has produced five hogsheads of sugar per acre. Last year the sand reef of Woodly Park, on the Berbice Coast, produced forty tierces of good sugar from five acres."

Mr. Joseph Gibbs in a report to Mr. Tinne and other gentlemen connected with British Guiana, dated August 18th, 1851, thus accounts for the advantage of thorough over ill-drained land. " If land is not drained down to the lowest root of every plant which grows in the soil, the plant cannot long continue in a healthy condition ; for it is obvious that no useful plant grows in a soil, the sub-waters of which are in a state of stagnation ; nor can any plant grow to perfection when the water which exists in the drains is not in a state of circulation, even if an excess of water be useful to such plant ; it is also essential to good cultivation, that if water be used for irrigation, it be applied to the surface, and be allowed to sink periodically through the soil with the atmosphere, the atmospheric penetration, and the aëration of the water applied to the roots of plants being essential to the healthful vigour of the plant, and being also an indispensable means of preventing the plant from being subject to periodical disease ; and these favourable conditions can only be accomplished in a swampy country by good drainage.

" To illustrate in the fewest words and in the most simple manner, the effect produced on land by draining it, and the opposite effect of its being saturated with water, it is only requisite to state, that if land is in a state of agricultural perfection, the water descending periodically through the soil, must draw after it the air, or the water could not descend ; now in dry weather, and during the day, water ascends by capillary attraction to the surface, and is evaporated out of the soil, though a small portion towards evening and during the night is recondensed ; it consequently forms a transitory void in the ground, by which the air can again enter, but as the water so ascending can only evaporate in its simple

* " Suggestions relative to the Improvement of the British West India Colonies," pages 70, 71· London: Bosworth.

state, it follows, that all the matters with which it is combined are left for the plant to feed upon; and as evaporation in the day and condensation at night produce alternate changes, in the displacing of the air by vapour and re-attracting it again to fill the vacuum, we perceive a process going on both during wet and dry weather, by night and by day, through which nutriment and vitality are given to plants below the earth's surface, conjointly and coincidently with the administrative functions of the air above.

" These considerations will sufficiently explain the importance of agricultural drainage preceding all other operations for causing a free action to be given to the elements which promote vegetable growth; and it is to these favourable circumstances, either existing in nature or produced by artificial processes, which assist nature in the elaboration of the soil, that those productions on which the human race and animals subsist, owe their perfection.

" Admitting the correctness of these observations, you will then be assured that a great increase of produce will follow the adaptation of every improvement in drainage, and that the increased produce will be of an infinitely greater commercial value than the cost of the improvement."

Mr. Gibbs concludes a very able paper by remarking, that " considering the unequalled fertility of the colony of Demerara,—considering, also, the vast sanitary improvements these works would accomplish,—and lastly, considering the adaptation of the climate for producing in the greatest abundance, and almost unequalled quality, the colonial merchandize required by Europe, if it be a duty on the part of the British Government to protect, extend, and foster the West India possessions at all, then it becomes an imperative duty to see that these improvements are carried out, by the enactment of such laws, and by the giving such aid, as may be necessary to give full effect to the measure."

I think your Lordship will not require further evidence or inducement to enable the free-labour cultivators of the British West India Colonies to thorough-drain their estates, and thus render them productive and profitable. To do this, that which seems necessary and practicable, is the application of the 9 & 10 Vict., c. 101, to the West India Colonies.

The effect of that application would be, as I apprehend, the use, on almost every sugar and cotton estate, of the draining plough, which has been used with so much advantage on the estate of His Royal Highness Prince Albert, at Windsor; of Lord Portman, in Somersetshire and Dorsetshire; the Duke of Buckingham, in Bucks; Sir Edward Buxton, in Essex; Lord Somers, in Herefordshire, and many other practical agriculturists, who have borne testimony to its economy and efficiency. (See Appendix.)

To judge of the applicability of the same machinery to the soil of British Guiana, a number of practical and disinterested men, who have been, or are, connected with the West Indies, have, within the past week visited the farm of Mr. Matthews, near Maldon, where the draining plough is at work, and the following are the opinions they have been led to form, by personal inspection and inquiry.

London, April 25th, 1853.

THE undersigned, who have been long resident in British Guiana, and practically employed in the management of sugar estates having been called upon to examine the draining plough invented by Mr. Fowler, and now at work in a field near the Maldon station, and to state their opinion as to its applicability to the soil and requirements of British Guiana, report as follows :—

The draining plough appears to be admirably adapted to the thorough drainage of the estates in that country, which are for the most part level and free from stone.

The land on which we saw the plough at work is a stiff clay, indeed stiffer than the clay lands of Guiana.

We have some doubts as to the practicability of finding horses who could bear the constant work in the tropics ; although oxen might answer. A portable steam-engine would seem best adapted for use in the colonies; especially as there is an abundance of wood for fuel growing on the sea-board of many of the coast lands.

Experiments made in Demerara by Dr. Shier, and mentioned in reports to the governor, published in the parliamentary returns from the sugar-growing colonies, in 1848 and 1852, have sufficiently established the fact, that not only is the crop of sugar made from thorough-drained land much greater in comparison with the crops on surface-drained, or imperfectly-drained land—but the quality also is greatly improved.

It apears to us, therefore, that one among other means of relieving the sugar growers of the West Indies from the difficulties of which they complain, would be that of enabling them by means of this plough to thorough-drain the land, and thus to improve the quality and increase the quantity of their sugar.

We conceive that a plough, or, if required, a subsoil plough, or scarifier, might be attached to the same machinery; by which means the land would be fitted for planting after draining; and thus the demand for hands to prepare the land for planting as well as making drains, would be lessened, or the quantity of land in cultivation increased.

The cost of thorough-draining in British Guiana, has been estimated at from £8 to £15, and even more, per acre; and it has been found, on experiment, to answer; but could not be effected to a great extent at these prices.

Although much better acquainted with the soil of British Guiana than either of the other West India Colonies, we see no reason to doubt that the draining-plough and scarifier would be equally useful in the level and alluvial soil of the other sugar-producing colonies.

GEORGE DANCKET, Manager for some years of Plantation "La Bonne Intention," and 29 years resident in the Colony of Demerara.

G. T. TAYLOR, Manager of Plantations "Mara," "Highbury," and "Zuidwick," Berbice, and 24 years resident in the Colony.

Having accompanied Messrs. Dancket and Taylor and other gentlemen on three occasions to witness the operations of Mr. Fowler's draining machinery; and having also during my residence for thirteen years in the West Indies paid much attention to the subject of drainage, I can have no hesitation to express my full conviction that they have rather under, than over, stated the advantages that may be anticipated from the general adoption of Mr. Fowler's draining plough.

STEPHEN BOURNE.

London, April 25th, 1853.

I have not had the advantage which the other gentlemen have had of personal examination of the land and cultivation in the West Indies, but from the reports of others and an inspection of the draining plough at work at Maldon, I am led to the conviction that Mr. Fowler's draining plough will be found of great advantage to the proprietors of land and the cultivators of the sugar-cane in Jamaica, &c.

J. M. WEBSTER, 46, Lime Street.

We witnessed, a few days ago, the operation of Mr. Fowler's draining plough on Mr. Matthew's farm, near Maldon, Surrey ; and readily bear testimony to its admirable efficiency. The drains were afterwards opened in our presence in two different places, and nothing could exceed the regularity and
pipes were found to be laid. The soil was a stiff clay

We are decidedly of opinion that Mr. Fowler's plough is calculated to be of very great use in the drainage of the alluvial soils of British Guiana, as well as of the lands of the other West India Colonies, where no rocks or other obstacles occur, and where the soil is firm.

The experiments of Dr. Shier of Guiana, although they cannot be cited for their economical results, owing to the disadvantages under which they were made, are yet valuable as demonstrating the considerable increase of quantity, and improved quality, of the produce of the cane in thorough-drained land. And we cannot doubt that, however satisfactory the results of thorough drainage in the agriculture of England, results still more satisfactory may be obtained from its use in tropical countries, which so frequently suffer from excess of rain as well as from droughts, especially when these succeed an unusually wet season. We are of opinion, however, that to insure the success of thorough drainage in the low lying coast lands of Guiana, it will be necessary to aid the existing outfall by means of machinery, to prevent the water in the large drains from rising above the level of the draining pipes.

D. Denoon, 6, Adams Court, London.
A. Denoon.

47, *Alfred Road, Westbourne Green, April* 27, 1853.

Having inspected Mr. Fowler's draining plough at work, and examined the drains, I am happy to be able to give my testimony as to its excellence, both as regards simplicity of construction, great power, and the effective manner in which the work is accomplished. The tiles are deposited with great regularity and exactness, far surpassing those laid by hand. With the addition of a steam-engine in lieu of horse power—and that is in the course of construction—this draining plough will be invaluable in all level and alluvial soils, but more especially in the tropical and sugar-growing colonies; such as Guiana, &c., where deep and sufficient drainage is indispensable. Its invention at this particular era cannot be otherwise regarded than as a gracious and providential dispensation to aid those colonies, and to advance the black population to the state of skilled husbandmen, by the use of implemental husbandry.

The one thing now required is, that England should consider her West India Colonies as integral parts of the Empire, and extend to them the benefit of the Draining Land Act. Such a step could not fail to enhance greatly their social and commercial condition, and to exhibit free negroes in such fair colours, as would enlist the sympathies, and excite the desires of slave-holding States, to imitate the philanthropic course of England.

John S. Osborn.

The petitioners from British Guiana (and amongst them the Chief Justice, himself an extensive proprietor and experienced planter) state, that the number of hands required to cultivate 100 acres of land with the sugar-cane, on the present plan, is fifty.

According to Governor Barkely's report to the Colonial Office, published in the Parliamentary returns for 1852, there were 36,271 acres of land cultivated with canes to produce 46,335 hogsheads of sugar. This, then, would require 18,145 labourers, according to the statement of the petitioners.

To defray the expense of introducing this number of labourers from the East Indies, and paying the passage of half of them back, would require a capital of £544,350. According to the estimate of the same petitioners, twelve men instead of fifty (for 100 acres) would be required, if aided by cattle and implemental labour on thorough-drained land. To cultivate 36,271 acres of canes in order to make 46,335 hogsheads of sugar by such aid, would require 4,400 labourers, that is less by 13,700; the capital required on their introduction would be therefore less by FOUR HUNDRED AND ELEVEN THOUSAND POUNDS than under the present system.

To thorough-drain this land by Mr. Fowler's steam draining plough, could not cost more than one hundred and fifty thousand pounds, and would last for twenty years. Two hundred and sixty-one thousand pounds of capital would thus be saved, whilst, according to the estimate both of the Governor and Dr. Shier, double, or even treble, the quantity of sugar, and that of a superior quality, might be safely calculated upon as the result. Thus the security for repayment, as well as the relief of the colonies from temporary embarrassment, would be promoted by the adoption of this plan; and what is of still greater importance, the draining of the coast lands would render the colonies healthy, and therefore desirable settlements for voluntary emigrants with, or without, capital.

In a Pamphlet recently published by Mr. Bosworth,* it is most clearly shown, that all attempts to increase the population in order thereby to reduce the price of labour in a country where land is so abundant and so cheap as in Guiana and Jamaica, must be delusive. The moment a man can save ten dollars, he will of course purchase therewith a freehold, and devote a portion of his time to its improvement. It is only by improved cultivation, and reduced expenditure, that the estates can be rendered productive, or borrowed capital repaid. When the people were slaves the case was different, but even then, the prosperity was rather imaginary than real. One in a hundred might prosper, but the mass were always in wretchedness, as must ever be the case where slavery exists. We may cheat our fellow-man, but cannot successfully trample under foot the laws of our Creator. The colonists never had other than one interest, and that was and is heartily to co-operate with the Queen, Government, Parliament, and people of the mother country in their attempts to establish on a firm foundation, free labour and free trade, and thus to present a successful example to all the slave-holding countries of the world.

The gentlemen who form the Jamaica Association are anxious for a large emigration of labourers, and relief from public debt. On these subjects I may hereafter take the liberty of making a suggestion or two; but I suppose all parties will agree in the opinion, that before any government can take upon itself to introduce a large number of emigrants into such a country as Jamaica is at present, they must know that there is at least a disposition on the part of the local government and the legislature to render the country fit for emigrants, by draining the coast lands. If this were done, both capital and emigrants of skill and industry would rapidly flow into our West India Colonies. Until it has been at least set about in good earnest, it will, I apprehend, be difficult to induce Parliament to agree, either to pay off old scores or to repeat experiments, the results of which it is fearful to contemplate.

With regard to the cultivation of cotton, it may be only necessary to remark, that the finest cotton ever imported in quantity into England, has been grown on the coast lands of British Guiana; and that the women and children of the free labourers in the West Indies would, if the coast lands were cleared and thorough-drained, supply a very large proportion of the cotton now in demand for our northern manufacturers, whose manufactured articles they would take in return for their raw material. British Guiana alone is a hundred thousand square miles in extent, and would, if it were cleared, drained, and cultivated, become healthy and attractive to the freed Africans, now resorting to Canada or remaining in the United States. A cold country never can suit the African race so well as the West India Colonies, which seem as well adapted for them as they are for the climate.

* "Suggestions relative to the Improvement of the British West India Colonies."

At an infinitely less expense than that which has been incurring for some years past, in order to obtain labourers from the East Indies and Africa, the use of cattle and implemental labour might thus be secured, and by a vast increase of the crops of sugar and cotton, as the consequence, the West Indies might regain, under the system of free labour and free trade, more than their former degree of prosperity.

There are three considerations to which I will further, for brevity's sake, merely advert :—

1. Emigration at the public expense has been a cause of great dissatisfaction to those who did not immediately benefit by it. Assistance by the Government on the security of estates, would be popular with every person in the colonies.

2. A training of the African and Cooly race in agricultural science and implemental husbandry, would enable those of them who may return to their native lands to assist in the regeneration of their own people.

3. Something like a return or compensation might thus be made by England to that deeply injured race whose enslavement and degradation former Governments have encouraged. Who that observes the signs of the times, can doubt that the Almighty is even now working out the improvement and elevation of the down-trodden races of men? The true wisdom of the governors of this great country is, not to obstruct, but to move on, in harmony with such gracious designs, and, by a noble example, to diffuse the light of Heaven.

These remarks have been chiefly made in reference to British Guiana, in which country I resided for nearly seven years, and expended much capital in attempts to drain an estate with a view to cotton cultivation. To that country the draining plough of Mr. Fowler is especially adapted ; but I have no doubt the greater part of the lands in all our West India Colonies, which are on the sea coast, would be rendered fertile and productive of sugar and cotton, as well as an abundance of provisions, if they were thorough-drained ; and with their comparatively scanty population, this can only be done by some such machinery as the draining plough. There are thousands of acres of land on the sea coast of Jamaica which might be made to produce three hogsheads of sugar per acre (which would, at the present short price, realize £45 to the grower), now lying in fallow, or covered with what is called bush. I apprehend that it is the same in Trinidad, Dominica, and St. Vincent ; probably in all the other Islands. Could these lands be put into cane and cotton cultivation we should soon cease to depend on the slave-holding states of America for cotton, or on Cuba and Porto-Rico for sugar. On the contrary, we might soon supply the continental markets with sugar. Slavery cannot last much longer. By rendering our own colonies prosperous, and proving the superior advantage of free labour, we may give the death blow to the accursed system of slavery in the new world.

I believe it to be in the power of the Government over which your Lordship presides, to bring about such a consummation ; and as I have a firm conviction that you have the will, I have not hesitated to endeavour, by these suggestions, to call attention to the means.

I have the honour to be, My Lord,
Your Lordship's very faithful and obedient servant,
STEPHEN BOURNE.

Brixton, Surrey, April 27, 1853.

APPENDIX.

Report from the undersigned, at His Royal Highness Prince Albert's Farm, Windsor.

Windsor, November 6th, 1852.

We, the undersigned, have this day inspected the land at Shaw Farm, Windsor, in the occupation of his Royal Highness Prince Albert, which was drained in January last, with " Fowler's Patent Draining Plough," and we find that the drains are working well.

Mr. Charles S. Cantrell, the late occupier of the farm, and Mr. Gravatt, the present bailiff, both report the land as much improved thereby.

(Signed)   WILLIAM TRUMPER, Dorney.
                FRANCIS SHERBORNE, Bedfont, Middlesex.
                CHARLES S. CANTRELL, Jun., Riding Court, Datchett, Bucks.
                JOHN NASH, Langley, Bucks.
                GEORGE TILLYER, Feltham.
                JOHN MERCER, Uxbridge.

From General Wemyss, Clerk Marshal to his Royal Highness Prince Albert.

To the foregoing report I perfectly agree (though unable to be present at the inspection), and wish to add the following remarks :—

The field, consisting of ten acres, was down in Clover Lay, and the operation of the plough did not disturb the surface in the slightest degree, the windlass working in one corner of the field ; and, excepting the main drains, which were cut by hand, no one would suppose from the undisturbed state of the surface, that a drain had ever been put in ; though the field was drained one rod apart, and three feet six inches deep, consequently the plough can be strongly recommended for grass and clover lands. The subsoil of this field is a strong retentive clay, and the top soil a mixture of clay and gravel about four feet deep.

(Signed)   J. WEMYSS.

Orchard Portman, March 2nd, 1853.

DEAR SIR,—Yours of the 28th ult. came duly to hand, and in answer I beg to say that the work done on my farm by your draining plough has given me great satisfaction.

Although we did upwards of seventy acres in about ten weeks, and more than fourteen months have elapsed since the work was completed, I have discovered no sign of any portion being out of order—that drained without pipes appearing, as yet, quite equal to the other where pipes were used.

I have no hesitation in recommending your implement for draining lands composed of a tenacious clay, with but few stones, and where there is an easy, but sufficient drainage fall, similar to that on my farm.

Under such circumstances it works with great efficiency, and the pipes are deposited with as much accuracy as if laid in by the hand of an experienced workman.

I am, dear Sir, yours truly,

To Messrs. Fowler and Co. HENRY BLANDFORD.

Sandridge, Bromham, Chippenham, Wilts, March 2nd, 1853.

GENTLEMEN,—In reply to your questions as to my knowledge of the use of your draining plough, I beg to state that my experience extends over a period of two years and a half.

I had some pasture land on the Kimmeridge clay, drained at distances of 33 feet, and to the depth of 3½ feet; it then struck me that the expense of the pipes may be saved in land of this description, and accordingly I made the experiment on one acre of land, and this I have from time to time inspected, and my own opinion and that of the tenant is, that the portion executed *without pipes*, is equally effective with that portion on which pipes were used, and the whole work, amounting to 24 acres, has acted in a satisfactory manner. The mains were laid in by hand labour.

I have this year had 75 acres, principally pastures, drained at a like distance, and though the clay on my farm is particularly tenacious, I find the drains to operate satisfactorily.

I have in addition to these works, which were on lands under my own management, had an opportunity of inspecting some work executed by your draining plough, on a deposit of gravel and silt, *debris* of the lias formation under clay, this has proved perfectly efficient, and the tenant, Mr. Blandford, of Orchard Portman, near Taunton, Somerset, is very much pleased with the effect produced on the land.

I am, Gentlemen, yours truly,

Messrs. Fowler and Co. HENRY BLANDFORD.

2, *Bolton Row, March* 14*th,* 1853.

DEAR SIR,—Having since I last wrote, had the opportunity to ascertain by personal inspection the state of the drains drawn by your plough in the course of the last summer and autumn, at Doddershall, I am glad to be able to state, that as yet they are perfectly efficient; the water still running freely at the outlets, and the ground above, notwithstanding its tenacious nature and the continued rains, being sufficiently dry to admit of bean setting and general tillage.

The only place in which the drainage has at all failed, is in a space of about 200 square yards, in the field next to the brick kiln, which was the first drained; the water was still lying there when I saw it, in the furrows. It is right, however, to add, that this may be accounted for, by the fact that this is the lowest part of the field, which has lately been altered in shape, and the furrows which a year since ran in one direction, having been altered to another direction, the surface is not quite level as yet. On the whole I am satisfied with the result hitherto, especially as the drainage is made without tiles; and I am of opinion that the cost will be nearly repaid in the crops of the first year.

I am, dear Sir, yours faithfully,

GRENVILLE PIGOT.

Messrs. Fowler and Co., Bristol.

From Mr. T. Scott, Agent to J. Neeld, Esq., M.P.

Messrs. Fowler and Co., Bristol.

Grittleton, Chippenham, Wilts, July 13th, 1852.

Sirs,—In answer to your inquiry, I am disposed to think that your draining plough will ultimately answer its intended end, by becoming, through practice, adapted to almost every clay and medium subsoil in the three kingdoms. I carefully watched and tested its progress while doing the one hundred acres at Braydon, and inspected the drains during and after the late heavy rains, and am satisfied with their efficiency and security; and if they are secure, of course, they must be permanent; at least, I am of opinion that by beginning at a depth of three feet, and going deeper in proportion to the increased porosity of the soil, they will last a life-time.

Your contract prices settle the question of economy; they being about one-half those paid for similar work done by hand.

I have seen many attempts at draining by machinery during the last thirteen years, in which I have almost constantly engaged in extensive works of drainage; but I do not think any invention has come within sight of yours in its adaptation to the end to be attained.

I am, Sirs, your obedient servant,

THOS. C. SCOTT.

From Mr. H. E. Parsons, Lord Portman's Steward.

To Messrs. Fowler, Harris, and Taylor.

Gentlemen,—In reply to your letter respecting the drainage done by your ploughs, I have much pleasure in saying, that since the late rains the drains are working well, and, at present, I have every reason to be perfectly satisfied with the work. I can already see a difference in the pasturage of the large field where the ploughs were the first set to work, as the cattle are feeding it much closer.

There have been upwards of 300 acres done on Lord Portman's property this spring under my inspection; the greater portion without pipes. On the Farm I am occupying under his Lordship there have been about 175 acres done,—the whole without pipes,—which I find has cost less than —— per acre, including horse-hire (but not main drains, which were cut by our own people); the drains were from 18 to 30 feet apart, according to soil, and 3 feet deep. Several fields with growing crops of wheat and vetches were drained, in April, without injury; and I consider the neatness and expedition with which your machines get through the work a great additional recommendation.

I remain, Gentlemen, Yours truly,

H. E. PARSONS.

Haselbury, Crewkerne, 8th July, 1852.

From Edmund Ruck, Esq.

Castle Hill, near Cricklade.

Dear Sir,—In answer to your inquiries with respect to the working of your Draining Plough, I have no hesitation in saying that I consider it an exceedingly valuable and efficient implement, and one which from its simplicity any ordinary workman can manage. On my lands the subsoil is a stiff clay, and I have not thought it necessary, generally, to put in tiles; but whenever I have used it for that purpose the tiles have been buried better than they can be laid by hand, which I have proved by taking up pieces of the drains. The saving effected by your machine is very considerable; the average quantity of work done being about 300 rods of 16½ feet per day.   *   *   *   *   *   *   On my stiff clay land I have thought it best not to drain more than 2½ feet deep; but I consider the Plough quite equal to 4 feet drainage in moist soils. I have now drained about 100 acres with your machine, and feel quite satisfied with the result.

Yours faithfully,

EDMUND RUCK.

From Collinson Hall, Esq.

Prince's Gate, near Brentwood, Essex, July 5th, 1851.

DEAR SIR,—In reply to yours of the 2nd inst., requesting my candid opinion of your Patent Draining Plough,—having now completed nearly 200 acres with it, I feel justified in strongly recommending it. I find the work much better executed;— that it is impossible (without gross neglect in the attendant), but that the pipes should be deposited in a cavity as true in its inside as a gun-barrel: and as a conse- quence, I think the drain will continue its purpose until the tile again returns to its original condition of clay. This will depend entirely on the quality of the tile, burn- ing, &c., and is quite independent of your invention.

Having, since Michaelmas last, taken three Farms greatly in want of drainage, my earliest consideration was to effectually drain them, and at the *smallest cost*. I had seen, about Christmas last, the drawings of your implement in the Illustrated Weekly Times, and I thought from them I ought to see the implement at work; and from that time its value has been well proved, by the work being executed in a very stiff and rather flinty marl, 2 feet 2 inches below the furrow (as nearly as I can calculate), for 2s. 3d. per score rods; paying three men 12s. per week, a boy 6s., and the horse- time 3s. per day.

I am so fully convinced, from the very sound character of this soil, that the cavity, which is egg-shaped, about 5 inches by 4 inches, and 2 feet 2 inches deep, with a very good fall,—will continue its shape and character—say for twenty years—that of late I have not inserted the pipes (although my landlord would pay for them), pre- ferring occupying my horse-time in making *two* of these drains or cavities instead of *one*; the one half of the horse-time being previously occupied in drawing the pipes a distance of four miles from this Farm. By this plan I have double the draining surface, with the same horse power, which, as a tenant for twenty-one years, on *this* soil, I think to be my best policy; hoping to induce my landlord to expend the value of the tiles in erecting some buildings a little in conformity with the age we live in, —not dark, damp, dirty, and, as a consequence, charged with foul air.

In conclusion; many gentlemen, owners and occupiers, have been here to see its work—each and all agree as to its accuracy.

Yours truly,

COLLINSON HALL.

From Mr. Oakley, Earl Somers' Agent.

Bronsia, near Ledbury, August 9th, 1852.

GENTLEMEN,—With the manner in which your Draining Plough has done its work on Lord Somers' Estate I am well satisfied, and thoroughly believe that for a large portion of this kingdom it is well adapted, particularly to the clay lands, which may be drained without tiles.

I consider, in land free from rocky stone, your Plough will cut its drains and lay the tiles at 3 feet 3 inches, in a superior style, and at a cost of 20s. per acre less than the cost by hand labour. This alone should command attention to your implement.

The cost of tiles saved, and invested at 4 per cent., would produce the cost of re-

cutting the drains in a few years,—I think long before it will be required. I therefore strongly incline, in stiff clay lands, not to use tiles.

Yours faithfully,

JOHN OAKLEY.

Messrs. Fowler, Harris, and Taylor.

From Mr. Beard, Agent to His Grace the Duke of Buckingham.

Stowe, near Buckingham, August 10, 1852.

DEAR SIRS,—I am in the receipt of your letter of yesterday's date. You ask me
for a prompt reply thereto, and which I readily give you.

I have had most extensive experience in draining in various counties for full forty
years, and *I confidently assert that by no other process have I seen drain-pipes so well
put into the ground as by your* DRAINING PLOUGH, which, I must think, will super-
sede every other mode of draining heavy lands for surface-water. I have so much
confidence in it, that I now ask the price of one complete, of the same strength, and
bores of the same calibre, as the one used at Wootton, as I shall persuade the Marquis of Chandos to buy one.

I am, your obedient Servant,

THOS. BEARD.

To Messrs. Fowler, Harris, and Taylor, Temple Gate, Bristol.

From Mr. H. Hickman, Bailiff to Capt. Blaine.

SIR,—In reply to your application to me for my opinion as to the efficiency of the
draining done by you for Capt. Blaine, in Winkfield Park, with Fowler's Plough,—I
can assure you it exceeds my expectations. The drains are now running a very full
stream; and a very perceptible difference is made as to the firmness of the surface as
you walk over the part under the influence of the draining.

The two great recommendations in favour of your method of draining over hand-
labour I consider to be—the great saving of expense; and, in grass lands, the not
disturbing the surface, which is so great an evil and eye-sore in hand-draining.

I am, Sir, Your obedient Servant,

HENRY HICKMAN.

Hawthorn-Hill, near Maidenhead, June 24, 1852.

From Mr. Thomas T. Clarke.

SIR,—It gives me great pleasure to be able to add my testimony to the valuable
services your draining plough is adapted to effect in our heavy clay lands. Though
of course, from the dry weather that succeeded the operations of the implement, I
am unable to speak of the vast amount of water that must have been given off had
the ground been saturated with rain—still the economy, rapidity, and neatness in the
execution is beyond all praise. I conceive that in stiff clay *meadow* land the draining would stand well for years, without tiles, where the land possesses a good *fall;*
as, of course, if the water is liable to be backed up the drains by floods, the arch of
the channel is softened and must fall in. Where this liability occurs I should recommend tiles to be put in, for a certain length, until the requisite fall can be procured.
The ease with which this can be performed—indeed, the simplicity of the machine
altogether, the little disturbance it causes upon the grounds,—makes it, in my
humble opinion, a first-class implement for the agriculturist.

Yours obediently,

THOS. T. CLARKE.

Swakelegs, July 10, 1852.

For EU product safety concerns, contact us at Calle de José Abascal, 56–1°,
28003 Madrid, Spain or eugpsr@cambridge.org.

www.ingramcontent.com/pod-product-compliance
Ingram Content Group UK Ltd.
Pitfield, Milton Keynes, MK11 3LW, UK
UKHW012339130625
459647UK00009B/395